THE
OUTSIDE
Observer

Surviving Your Loved One's
Addiction Through Spirituality

Written and Channeled by
Patricia Horton
A Medium at Heart

We will all cross the great divide one day, and leave a life well lived behind us. It does not mean that the life we lived no longer matters. It just means that we have given, learned, and grew while here. It is when our contract is fulfilled that God will call us home. Yet the breadcrumbs left behind by us, become the essence of our existence.

The Outside Observer
Surviving Your Loved One's Addiction Through Spirituality

Book Design by Transcendent Publishing
ISBN: 979-8-9931662-9-2

Disclaimer: Although the author and publisher have made every effort to ensure that the information in this book was correct at press time, the author and publisher do not assume, and hereby disclaim, any liability to any party for any loss, damage, or disruptions caused by errors or omissions, whether such errors or omissions result from negligence, accident, or any other cause. The publication is meant as a source of valuable information for the reader, and discernment on the reader's part is advised. The use of this book implies your acceptance of this disclaimer.

Printed in the United States of America

ACKNOWLEDGMENTS

I want to give credit to God and all His Glory. He has provided me with the gift of being the scribe and the strength to share my own story of how addiction has touched my family.

The promise of peace restored is given, if only I allow.

He has shown me that by honoring myself in the process, it will help to heal my personal brokenness.

My wish through my writing, is to help others on the same journey.

DEDICATION

I dedicate this book to all the addicts on this side of life and the other. Through your journey of addiction, I have learned so much. Not only about myself, but you as well.

The toughest part being, how to survive your battle. How to move through life as I have loved and watch you struggle. How to maintain and smile while my heart breaks along the way.

I have no idea what led you to your addiction, and I often wonder why. Why this drug? Why that choice? Why has the pathway towards healing been so difficult for you?

Not only do you need to heal, but so do I.

At times my worry, my fears, my thoughts have made me feel isolated. Today I decided it was time to put into words a journey of two separate souls navigating one path: addiction. Today is the day that I honor you. This is where I thank you for showing me that through your own journey, I have found a way to help others.

Together, we will discover that addiction is only the tip of the iceberg. Buried deep beneath the rubble, peace is waiting for all of us, and most deservedly, our addict.

My words, my thoughts, my own personal experiences, will be the tools that I share. I share them to help others who have not yet found the ground beneath their feet to navigate this long and winding road.

I know that you are more than your addiction, and I am more than the person who is battling it along with you. You are and have always been special.

My hope is that each person who reads this book can remember this as well about their own loved one.

IN REMEMBRANCE OF

*Please know it is through the hearts of the living, that
the departed make their presence known.*

*For this is the place where the memories of a life
shared between you both reside.*

*It is from within the heart, where the love between
you is felt the deepest.*

*And it is through your love for one another that the
connection is still very much alive.*

Channeled January 5, 2019

*A*s I sit in reflection of all things you, my love and prayers become
the peace needed as I navigate a World without you in it.

*The smiles come in waves, as my memories of you give me hope,
that we will be reunited once again when my own time comes.*

*It is from a deep sense of faith and prayers, said in your honor,
that I know you have been healed of those things that you could not
find the strength to heal on your own.*

And it is in God's Hands that I know you reside, as He Holds You in His Loving Embrace.

It is never goodbye. It is always until we meet again, in this world or the next, as your love continues to teach me from this side of life.

I have added your name to the list below, as I know each time these pages are visited, your light will continue to shine.

In Remembrance of

Thomas "Tommy" Horton

Justin Millhorn Sr.

Chester "Chuck" Horton

Robinson "Robbie" Bourget

Marky "Uncle Buck" Williamson

James "Jay" Millhorn

Kevin S

Darby S

Kevin J

Micheal Y

Perry Pesek

Jordon Vogel

Patty Simpson

Joey V

Gilley

Harlon P

Jessica Rose F

Danny S

Michael Dean Otis Jr.

Frank Cavaliere

John Z

Roger Z

Glenn Z

Bella

Courtney Young

Donald McBride

Phyllis Dawn Pelio

Deanne Robin Pelio Mazzarella

On the blank space below, please add the names of those you wish to be remembered.

For like a chalice, their names are lifted up to the Lord, and the prayer above is said in their honor.

CONTENTS

PREFACE
CHASING THE DRAGON

The Dragon's hold is like a boa constrictor.

As the drug becomes the elusive Dragon, the human being becomes lost.

Temporarily, the Dragon holds the reins while the human being's idea of reality has become skewed.

This is where the Dragon is worshiped as a god, and the drugs become the false idol glorified. Shortly after, reason falls to the wayside.

Human beings must break their own ties with the Dragon, even though the Dragon has become what they see as their life, or the way.

It is in the breaking of the ties that bind them, when, and before freedom is truly realized.

You see, the Dragon becomes the gatekeeper of the lesson that addiction offers, and it is the Dragon who holds much power over the will of the mind. Yet, it is through the will of the addict who creates a safe haven for the Dragon to dwell.

When the chains of addiction are removed and tethers cut, the Dragon's power ceases to exist any longer.

Yet, it is in the memory of the Dragon that becomes the constant reminder, and at times the lure back into the Devil's Den.

This is when the addict must choose life or death.

As the breath of life blows within them, it is realized by them, in glorious ways.

Channeled and Inspired Writing July 28, 2018

INTRODUCTION

I clearly remember hearing in the 1980s that every person would know someone who had died of AIDS, and/or contract the disease themselves. This was scary for everyone, but perhaps more so for very sensitive souls like me. Partly, it was because AIDS had so much stigma attached to it; partly, it was because the death of so many was a thought that my young mind could not process.

I never could have imagined that the real Dragon lurking in the background was drug addiction.

Who would have thought that it would run so rampant through the streets of America, and take so many lives? Who could have imagined that it would be available on every street corner? Who would have known that the internet would become a drug superhighway through which an addict could contact a dealer and purchase their dope?

Not me, that's for sure. I never realized that we would lose two-plus generations to the Dragon's grip. More importantly, I think it's high time that we find a way to kick the Dragon to the curb, or at least restore a place of peace for ourselves in the process.

Through my own journey with family and friends, I have come to realize that addiction has most likely touched everyone's life in some form or fashion. Young, old, female, male, the Dragon has sunk its talons into so many. Sadly, there is not one person living today who does not know someone in the throes of addiction.

Addiction touches the poorest of the poor to the richest of the rich. No one is immune to the Dragon's influence. The truth is, you don't even have to be using drugs to be trapped in the wicked web it has woven.

Let's take a look back in time, historically. In the 1800s, adultery was a crime for which people were punished in a variety of ways, including death. If you've read Nathaniel Hawthorne's classic novel, *The Scarlet Letter*, you know that the more "fortunate" adulterers were sentenced to a life of humiliation, by having to wear the letter A on their clothing to identify their crime. As I see it, addiction is this century's Scarlet Letter "A." The letter may not actually be visible, but the addict will carry the weight and the shame just the same.

As I stand on the sidelines, I become a witness to the addicts' plight. They walk around aimlessly, separated from hope, faith, and God. Their only source of comfort is coming from the Dragon himself. This is where I become an outside observer, and at times, one of the many people chasing their loved ones through the streets. As I try to reach my child through the fog of their addiction, I am left feeling helpless in the process.

People have a misconception that drug use only occurs on the streets and within broken homes. These same people will point their finger in your direction saying, "How could you have allowed this to happen? *My* kid would never touch drugs."

My response to them is, "How can you be so sure?"

Drug use starts in secret; the Dragon is hidden and silently gathering strength within your child. By the time it emerges, you no longer recognize the person standing before you. You, the "Outside Observer," will begin to do anything to try and save your addict, not yet realizing that the saving begins with themselves.

Whether you are an addict or the outside observer, addiction is one of the hardest lessons the soul comes back here to learn. Both sides are warriors, each lost in their own personal war. The addict is fighting that Dragon inside; the outside observer is literally fighting to save their loved one's life. They perceive this war differently because they are operating on two very different planes. One is high as a kite, and the other is sober as a church mouse. They will continuously intersect for brief moments at a time, before separating once more. It is a long and torturous journey, but a journey nonetheless.

I want you to know that all is not lost; and some addicts do recover. The reality on the backside of recovery is, they may fall again. An addict will always be an addict, and there will always be triggers that can potentially set them off. We may never know what those triggers are, yet they are a reality for the addict. The ups and the downs, the highs and the lows, are simply a part of the journey. This is the hardcore truth of how addiction and recovery work. A link between two realities, intertwined, and with addiction leading the way.

For the outside observer, life can feel like the worst amusement ride you have ever been on. Just when you begin to feel settled, you will find yourself upside down once more. At times, you may feel like you can't go on any longer, but this is precisely when you will dig deep and try again. Just when you think you have nothing left to give, you will find yourself back on the ride.

The words I will share with you now, come from the many leaders who work in the healing centers of recovery.

"As long as they have breath in their bodies, there is still hope."

Hold onto these words, because at times, they will be the only thing that makes sense.

Trying to save an addict is like trying to break into what you may see as an abandoned house. You don't have the key to the door, you don't hold the title to the home, and you don't retain the rights to the property. "Free Will" is the landlord here, and the addict has leased the property through this avenue. This is a contract that can only be canceled by them. You have to truly understand this truth to make it through.

In time, and after many attempts to break into this "abandoned house," I would come to accept this simple truth: every person, including the addicts in our lives, has free will. It is an ironclad gift from God, and no one, not even those with the best of intentions, can violate it.

Leaning on God, has become essential for me over the years. Most importantly, it has helped me come to a place of understanding and acceptance when it comes to addiction. With time on your part, I believe that you can get there too.

There are four possible outcomes when it comes to drug addiction:

Overdose.

Recovery.

Jail.

Death.

We all hope for that second outcome; however, there is no single solution that exists when it comes to addiction or recovery. It is hard to say what will work. Whatever happens, you will also go through the grieving process. Why wouldn't you? You are literally, symbolically, or both watching death happen before your very eyes. Grief through addiction works like this.

First stage: Denial

Second stage: Sadness

Third stage: Anger.

Fourth stage: Acceptance.

Throughout this book, I will share personal experiences with you about the addicts in my own life. I will show you how I navigated those experiences of active addiction and restored my own inner peace.

My intention is to help you navigate the world of addiction through my experiences and teach you how to find peace in the process. Again, central to finding peace, is accepting that free will is in play here. And it is through the free will of the outside observer where you can choose suffering or freedom.

I will also share with you the power of prayer and how to pray. As an outside observer, I am sure you have said a few. I will teach you that it is in the words spoken and intention set, where you will find comfort.

Ponder this for a moment: When we realize what we are truly praying for, and for whom, is when we give it to God as they say.

While I believe my words will be helpful, I also must stress to you that there is no one-size-fits all when it comes to addiction or recovery. Just as each addict will have their challenges, recovery is individual for each person. It is hard to say what will work. I encourage you to navigate this path with your addict and together if possible. This is where you will see how drug addiction affects all sides of the equation.

As we try to find compassion for the addict, an understanding for the outside observer is also important. The final piece to the puzzle is holding people (i.e., the addict) accountable for their own actions. Yes, the battle of addiction is real, and it may seem as if only the strong will survive. I can assure you that you each have a strength that is beyond measure.

In the end, addiction will leave its scars upon many. Some scars are deeper than others. When the scar does appear, place your hand over it and thank it for its wisdom. This scar becomes the reminder of what you have each gone through.

Most importantly, I will share what it means to have faith so you can understand its power, and recognize how it can carry you forth, even when it seems all hope is lost. It is through your faith where the miracles of life are birthed, even when you find yourselves standing on shaky ground. Finally, keep God on as your Wingman. You are going to need Him more than you know, as you try to navigate a situation that seems hopeless at times.

It is now time to move forward, together, and lean on faith as we heal our spirits along the way.

Faith Is An Unseen Force

From one dark cloud bursts 1000 rainbows, if only you can see beyond the parameters of the darkness.

As each of you know, faith cannot be seen nor touched.

It can only be experienced.

Your faith cannot be bought in a store, as it has no tangible container to hold it within.

Faith is that deep belief within you that does not need a fancy wrapper to know that it exists.

The foundation in your beliefs is where faith is born of. Once birthed, it will remain with you for a lifetime lived.

It is your faith that will deliver you to unopened doorways.

As you cross each threshold, you will know that your faith has delivered you home.

Channeled May 23, 2014

HOW TO READ THIS BOOK

This book will connect the spiritual aspect with the very human experience of addiction. I have found, that when you apply all aspects of your own soul's journey to the process of your everyday reality, you can see things more clearly. I am not saying it is going to be easy, because there is work to be done on your part as well.

The work revolves around finding your own footing in what has become uneven ground. This is where you will dig deep, get your hands dirty, while realizing that your blood, sweat, and tears, are all worth it in the end.

As I moved throughout this journey, there were many times when I fell backward; I too am only human. What I have realized, however, is that it was often in those moments of the push and the pull with my addict where I learned the most.

What you will experience during our time together is not a cure for your addict. This is a place where common ground is shared, knowledge gained, and wisdom applied by you. Again, your own free will is key to survival in this jungle we call addiction. It is through what we each learn about ourselves that becomes the prize in the end.

Allow this book to become a road map for you, and a place where we can all find common ground together. Each person who is in the midst of active addiction will find themselves at a different juncture in the life of their addict. Yet if desired, a healing for the outside observer can occur.

Throughout this book, I will be sharing channeled wisdom (in bold italics), inspired writings, and personal experiences of my own. At times, the channeled wisdom is given in parables. It is up to you to sit with those passages and gain personal knowledge for yourself.

Following some of the channeled passages, you will see what I call the Author's Reflections. This is where I will give you a peek into my own understanding of these messages and tools that can be applied through the lesson taught in that parable. This is where I will walk you to the threshold; it is up to you to step over it. Honestly, it is only when you are ready that all things are realized, understood, and where the truth can no longer be denied.

To this end, I suggest that you get a journal and put pen to paper. As you read, and re-visit those hard moments, you can document your own truth. There is value in your story, so write every moment down.

As you allow your story to present itself, capture any feelings coming to the surface. This is the point at which the true healing, understanding, and forward movement begin to present themselves. There is no detail too small to revisit.

There will also be a blank page at the end of several chapters where you can document your thoughts.

It is ultimately up to you to decide how you choose to navigate your personal journey through addiction. Knowledge is power, as they say, and this book can help you to discover this truth for yourself.

Author's Reflections

As we move forward, I wish to do so in love and in light.

I send to each person healing energy to use as you choose. I ask that God's Grace blanket you during your time of need.

I also pray that the wisdom gathered in these moments will be shared by you and with others who may find themselves standing in similar shoes. This is where the student becomes the teacher.

May the Grace of God's Glory rise within each of you and guide you forward. May you hear His voice, feel His love, and understand His wisdom for you, Amen.

I WILL SIT WITH YOU

We all have struggles in life, be it with family, addictions, depression, or even a lack of self-love. It is only when we begin to search for a light in the storm, when God will send us one in the form of an earth angel.

These earth angels are the people who sit with us through our dark moments. Through their love and grace for us, we have the ability to catch a glimpse of light. And it is from this light where the answers emerge.

Who have your earth angels been during the difficult moments of active addiction? Write them down in your journal, as they too become a part of your story.

With an addict, it seems as though the darkness will never subside.

Ponder this for a moment: the thread of addiction is connected to every outside observer, including you and I. These threads are where the roads of active addiction, previously traveled by you, become enlightenment. By sharing your journey is how you become an earth angel, a light for those who are navigating the darkness of addiction today. This is where your experiences become a platform to teach from.

As we all sit together for a time, supporting one another with God's grace becoming the gift, we eventually become a light for those who are navigating this same darkness. This is where the spirits of many are comforted.

Your earth angel during our time together will be your journal. It will become that shoulder to lean upon. That listening, nonjudgmental ear to hear. And most importantly, an avenue for unconditional love to swim within.

For the seeker or even the bearer of light, this is for you.

If you find yourself the seeker of another person's wisdom. Or even the giver of what is needed now.

Know that you both play a part in illuminating the darkness as you both share in one another's light.

Channeled and Inspired Writing

June 23, 2016

MEMOIR OF THE DIARIST

Journal your thoughts in the space below.

THE IMPORTANCE OF PRAYER

I spoke with you about prayer, and I am asking you to pin this page as you will travel back here often. Praying is so important as it gives you an opportunity to do something for your addict when you feel there is nothing more you can do in the flesh.

The power in prayer happens on a Universal level when the silent pray.

It is the power of those silent voices that change the world through belief, faith, and hope.

Channeled August 16, 2017

Hopelessness keeps you from your own internal peace. It detaches you from that Divine Spark within you. This Divine Spark is known as God.

When your hopelessness separates you from God, the Dragon begins to win on all fronts. It is through prayer that the Dragon is defeated, even for those who have forgotten, or maybe were never taught about the power of prayer.

Today, that changes, because learning to lean on God and praying for your addict is the one thing you are in control of. I use the word control here, because during active addiction "out of control" seems to be the norm.

In the middle of the night on August 16, 2018, I was woken up and given these words from God.

> *God will never let you down. He always has a hand extended to you when you need to be lifted up.*

Wow, I remember thinking, *That is powerful!* It was also what I needed to hear at that time, when my addict had been so heavily on my mind.

I pray for my addict daily, and before I close my eyes at night. When I see them struggling, I call upon a few extra favors in their honor.

The guidance given to me about prayer has always been...

> *When you pray for another person, their own soul is elevated towards the light.*

To me, this is what the power of prayer means on a grand scale. It provides me comfort during those difficult times. It took some time for me to understand that this is the only control I will ever have when it comes to my addict.

We all want to help those closest to us. Sometimes we forget that it's not up to us to fix them. But we can always pray for them. This is where the power of prayer comes in, and where your requests for that person is heard on a Universal Level.

Say A Little Prayer For Me

It is not what you say nor what you do that will change anyone. For change is a natural progression of the individual person, who is in need of change's influence.

Please know that it is when the person is ready to change that they will step forth to drink from changes cup, and not a moment beforehand.

No person, nor higher power, can ever infringe upon the free will of the learning soul. Yet, prayer does assist and will elevate those in need of your prayers.

God does hear all prayers, and He feels your yearnings when it comes to another soul. Yet, it is when the soul who is in need of your prayers, becomes open to receiving your prayers, where change happens.

Time and space given, delivered, and received.

Prayers are, in a sense, energy, sent by one person on behalf of another. This is the simple path on which prayers are assimilated by each person.

Please know that your prayers do assist in the transformation of the soul in need, as they move from one state of being and into the next. It is when this transformation occurs that miracles happen, and where your prayers become answered.

This is, after all, how prayer was meant to be realized by those who understand the power of prayers impact upon your brothers and your sisters.

Channeled March 19, 2017

Author's Reflections

I would like to share a quick prayer to use when you want to pray for someone in need.

It is important to remember that your prayers in that moment are for them, and not about you. This is where you remove yourself from the equation so the prayer can be fully received on a soul level.

When you pray the prayer shared below, insert the name of your addict into this prayer. This is where the words that you speak hold the vibration of love that you have for that person.

This is a powerful way to be heard even when your words feel as though they are falling on deaf ears. Your prayer then becomes an invisible gift, delivered through the breath of unconditional love. If accepted by the addict on a soul level, they can and will be transformed.

Dear God,

I ask that You draw near to my beloved (insert name) and whisper within his/her ear.

I ask that Your words pierce his/her heart and make way for his/her Divine Purpose to be revealed.

I ask for You to grant him/her Divine grace and a healing of the spirit as You intercede on his/her behalf.

I ask that Your voice is heard as it rises up from the darkness and reveals the light.

I ask that (insert name) be bathed in Your light so that he/she can find his/her way to better days.

I pray that (insert name) be delivered from the darkness of her addiction and renewed once more.

In the name of Jesus Christ I pray that Your will be done. Amen.

This prayer is filled with intent, and it is through your own heart's desire that you share this gift with someone on the receiving end.

Visit this prayer often and immerse yourself in God's Mercy as you pray for another.

Below is another prayer you may find comfort in.

A Prayer of Hope

Dear Child of Mine (your addicts name),

I love you deeply. My heart rejoices as I say your name, yet my spirit hurts when I see your struggle.

You have always been bright and inquisitive, with the tenacity to succeed.

Perhaps you have forgotten that. I want you to know that with God, all things are possible.

Stop seeing the roadblocks, the detours, the dead-end roads.

Change your perspective so that these things can be removed.

I want you to realize that you are more than your current set of circumstances.

If you so desire, your life can be healed, your spirit renewed, your heart reconciled with God.

Your life, in so many ways, has only just begun.

If only you would allow the beautiful wisdom of your own soul's voice to bubble to the surface. This is where it can become your tour guide moving forward.

As long as you are breathing the breath of life, hope and faith are willing to carry you over the threshold.

I will be on the other side, championing you forth.

Your choices, my prayers, God's Divine Intervention.

Inspired Writing February 3, 2024

THE ADDICT

The addict is a wily character and comes in many shapes and sizes. From young to old, man or woman, the choice to use was their own.

The addict will deny, steal, lie, and make excuses 'til the cows come home. They all use the same lines when they are busted, before turning it on you. They will blame you, accuse you, confuse you, and make you question your own sanity at times. They use this tactic as an escape route. This is where they can storm down the driveway, get in a stranger's car, and leave you standing there scratching your head while holding your heart in your hands.

After their departure, you may notice something of value has been taken from your home; most likely, it's your own peace. But, again, you stand there and do nothing. You justify it by saying, "That's my child and I want to help him/her," and the cycle continues.

This is when the addict disappears into the darkness, sometimes for days, while you're worried sick that they are going to die. When they resurface, you try not to bring up whatever happened before they left. This is when the addict knows they got you. This is the time in their addiction when they have positioned themselves as the victim and you as the aggressor.

It is the time when they may say, "It's your fault I use," or "Leave me alone, I like being high." They may even start a physical fight with you; then, on a dime, they will turn on the tears while looking for sympathy from others. They do it with such conviction that you again question yourself, even though you know they are lying.

This has been my experience with my addict.

Take a moment to write about your own experiences in your journal. It is through this exercise that you will capture the event and see the cycle of manipulation the addict is causing.

In time, you will realize that the trust between you has been broken. It will take great strides to restore it; it may even take years. During active addiction, the addict can only see their own wants and needs, with trust becoming an afterthought or not considered at all.

Despite your frustration, your love often becomes bigger than your anger. Women, more so than men, can be the weak link when it comes to the addict. This is true in my case. I did things to protect my addict because I knew my husband would not be so easily pushed around. First and foremost, I did this out of fear. I felt helpless in a fight I could not win. I kept silent, spun the truth, and even gave into demands so I would not lose touch with my addict. I had no idea what I was doing. I only knew that they needed me, and I was not ready to abandon this sinking ship.

In fact, this ship has been taking on water for ten years now. What a long time to be running the bilge pump! I have changed a few things from what I did in the beginning;

however, my unconditional love for my addict seems to always push itself forward, and there are times when I feel like I am back at day one.

How many of you have covered for your addict? This is when honesty matters and is what will put you on the pathway toward healing. Take a moment to write in your journal an example of that "cover-up," then move on. Dwelling on it will not change it, but shining a light on it can heal it.

The addict can be so irrational at times, that you may give into them out of fear for their safety. It is such a wicked game they play as the Dragon becomes the puppet master, pulling their proverbial strings. This is when some of us may pray and pray, to no avail. We begin to think, *Is God even listening?* I can assure you He is.

We have all seen addicts on the streets, yet how many of us ever expected to see it happen in our own homes? I can't help but think what a strange time this is. Kids and young people seem so lost, it's as if they are detached from their own internal compass. The sacred place within, that leads them to those purposeful moments in life. We watch in silence as their destiny is being squandered right before our very eyes, yet we go on for years in a cycle that serves only the Dragon.

Even as I write this, I find myself asking whether this is accurate. Maybe my addict's destiny during this life was to learn how to overcome, and mine was to teach from the outside observer's point of view. What I do know, is that whatever role you are playing in the journey, addiction can suck the life out of you.

When the addict is our child, we did our best to teach them the difference between right from wrong. After addiction takes its hold, we may find ourselves questioning, "Where did *I* go wrong?" This, my friends, is when we as outside observers, can become broken. In fact, we may not have done anything wrong, but we will never realize this truth until the recovery of our internal peace is achieved.

Stop for a moment and validate yourself in this process. At what stage do you find yourself today? Are you blaming yourself, and if so, why? Write down your thoughts in your journal and move on.

As I have seen in my own family, addiction can be generational. I am a witness to both alcoholics and hardcore drug users. The question is, what effect has the drunken or high behavior of an adult or even a sibling in your household had on the kids in your family?

Take a moment, grab your journal, and connect a few dots. Is addiction in your family generational, or did it show up unexpectedly? What do you deem the link to your own addict to be?

When facing the hard facts, including your role in the Dragon's game or your addict's story, is how can you begin to heal the broken pieces within yourself. You will likely realize and recognize that other areas of your life need attention as well. If they are abandoned for too long, the family as a whole suffers while the addict continues to dance with the Dragon.

If all we do is wait for that phone call, think the worst daily, and blame ourselves for their choices, we are not living the lives

God desires for us. We have instead become victims in the Dragon's game.

It boils down to this: it is all about choices. The addicts have made their choice, and their choices moving forward will determine their path through addiction or God willing recovery. In no event, however, should their choice to use ever dictate your own. The only way through addiction happens when the addict desires help.

In the end, all you can do is be a source of support. Be very careful here. There is a difference between supporting your addict and enabling your addict. This is where the lines can become blurred for the outside observer.

MEMOIR OF THE DIARIST

Journal your thoughts in the space below.

THE GREAT FALL

*As the serpent rises from the ashes. His movements
are slow and steady, deliberate and calculated.*

*He steps forth to test you, to entice you, to lure you
toward the darkness. It is through his wicked ways
that snares the innocent to wander towards and into
the underworld.*

*As you follow him, you may fall. Slipping further and
further away from the light.*

*God calls out. If they would only look up and towards
the heaven above, they would still see the light.*

*It is, after all, in the light of God's love for them, that will
lift them from the depths of their despair. It is within this
light that they are healed and made whole again.*

*As the serpent promises you heaven, it is by his promise
that he leads you to hell. And those who dwell within
his prison, know the true meaning of darkness.*

*Yet, it is within the prison of this darkness, that the
light of truth is born.*

Channeled January 4, 2015

Author's Reflections

This is a powerful message, and it speaks to those who have struggled or are struggling with addictions.

The sorrow we feel watching our addict use, with the drug of choice dictating the way, pains our hearts and where we are left feeling helpless, asking, What are we to do?

Prayer is one way that we can assist the addict. It is where we can help them on a soul's level. It is where we can aid in elevating the vibration of their soul through the words spoken.

The healing power of prayer is twofold, and we must remain honest during this painful time.

This is where we must come to realize the power of another person's free will. It is where we must recognize that we have no authority in the choices made by the addict.

By returning to prayer, we are given an avenue to help on a deeper and unforeseen level. This is something to be learned by all parties involved.

There is always going to be the next time, or another family affected by addiction. It is where we can share with them the power of prayer as they navigate this long and winding road of addiction themselves.

This is where the power of knowledge is applied through personal experience. It is our way of helping them break the fall.

Even though we have witnessed the dark side of addiction, we are each given an opportunity to grow due to the experience. It is also the place that we get to bear witness to God's love and grace.

FREE WILL OF THE ADDICT

When your soul chooses to walk upon the dark side of the moon, the light of the moon then becomes an illusion of the mind.

You see, the way to be fully immersed and bathed within her light, is to step away from the shadows. This is where you are being called to expose all that is Holy within you.

For as the snake slithers along, leading those who are weak into the shadows of this world. The hawk will then take away the snake's power by pulling it into the heavens above and consuming its evil ways.

Dwell not where fools dabble, and know that each step you take, is of your own Free Will.

Channeled April 24, 2015

Author's Reflections

This message speaks clearly to our addictive behaviors and what becomes a lesson for the addict on a soul level.

Please remember that addictions come in many shapes and sizes. Once recognized, they can then be broken.

Continue to pray for those who are weary, as it is through your love and prayers that the souls of others are elevated.

Even if you are not a praying person, during our time together give it a try. Become aware of how prayer makes you feel. It is through this process you can then experience the full power of God's Grace during your prayer time.

Make a note in your journal about the exercise of praying. You may be surprised by your own experience.

MEMOIR OF THE DIARIST

Journal your thoughts in the space below.

BROKEN TRUST

Trusting Soul are You.

For trust is born of heart energy and can be quite easy when it comes from a place of love.

As you question nothing, you are giving those you trust the freedom to live, and allowing them to just be.

This is where trust can become a slippery slope.

Don't become so blinded by trust that you end up blinded by the light of reality, and where you cannot see the forest through the trees.

Just remove the light from your eyes, and see the reality that is before you.

As you do this, you are given the slate of truth to lean upon.

It is in the energy of this truth that you are set free.

Channeled May 4, 2014

Author's Reflections

When it comes to an addict, truth and trust are easily broken.

This message is a reminder that while trust is an energy based on love, that energy can be used against us.

This is when we tend to fall on our sword, all in the name of love, while the addict continues to betray our trust.

We have to put safeguards in place and understand that trust needs to be earned. There comes a time, especially when active addiction is present, when it should not be given so freely. Never allow another to use your trust as a weapon against you.

JUDGE NOT, LEST YE BE JUDGED

This is for both the addict and the outside observer of addiction. Judgment can be a double-edged sword.

Sometimes we do things to the bewilderment of others. We do them because our free will, offers us the opportunity to learn from what we cannot see clearly, just yet.

Each of us has chosen addictions or an addict, and where we become attached to them for a lesson on a soul level. Most of the time, it is a family member who has come into our life out of a need for soul growth, or for karmic reasons. It can be a complicated road to travel, but this is the one we have chosen to evolve upon. If you're asking, "What is karma?" allow me to explain.

Karma Is The Teacher

Karma is the teacher and you the student.

Karma gifts you the opportunity to learn, grow, and move on in a different direction in life.

If you avoid Karma's Teachings, you will only suffer endlessly until you do.

Karma's voice cannot be denied.

You see, Karma offers you more than a kick in the pants. It offers you an opportunity for change within your lives.

Please know that it is only through change that you can alter the current course that you may be traveling.

When Karma offers you the chance to change directions, you must do so, or you will remain in the status quo of your current state of affairs.

Channeled May 21, 2015

What is the nature of the addiction or the addict you are dealing with presently, or have dealt with in the past? Are you on a continuous spin cycle, or have you recognized the need for change on your part? Change is not only for the addict here; it also applies to the outside observer.

Pause for just a moment and make an entry in your journal. Be honest with your answer. Write it all down and move forward when ready.

The wisdom of karma is realized on both sides of one coin. The beauty of the wisdom is that both the addict and the outside observer can benefit.

For the addict.

As you move forward, know this: there is no other person who can know your heart or the divinity of your soul's purpose.

*Yet those closest to you will try to guide you out of
love. They can even get angry out of frustration.*

*Yet you stay the course because you still have so much
to learn, as do they.*

Each of you has heard the saying, *"There is a reason for everything."* I believe this is true, yet you must remain mindful
of the fact that your own actions affect everyone and everything. Those closest to you may struggle as they try to understand your choices; this is when judgment makes its presence
known.

Yes, your stubbornness can be seen as willfulness and your
addiction may be viewed as a weakness. Yet no other person
really knows what has delivered you to your current situation.

Due to your actions, you may lose some people who were
at one time your closest allies. Why? Because they will never
be able to gain a complete and total understanding of the *whys*,
the *hows*, and the *whens*.

Please know that no one is immune to the challenges that
addiction will bring into your life.

As we move forward, here are some words for the Outside
Observer as well.

*With that in mind, you must remain vigilant against
judgment's intoxicating influence.*

*This is where she sits before you and offers you a sip of
her influential elixir.*

Each person living has been privileged to her wicked ways, yet the sweetness of the drink can become easy for us to swallow.

It is up to the participant whether or not to drink from her cup of judgment or peacefully pass it by.

Channeled April 16, 2016

Author's Reflections

Before you move on, look at your own life. This is where you will see which side of the fence you currently find yourselves standing on.

As you dig deep for compassion for others or for self, know that you have the strength to overcome.

This is where you can begin to remove the barriers so that understanding can be gained on a soul level.

These are important steps to be mindful of and worthy of your time.

Try not to rush forward, as the journey toward understanding and healing is worth your patience.

MEMOIR OF THE DIARIST

Journal your thoughts in the space below.

LET'S TALK ABOUT GRIEF

When someone dies, or it feels as if a part of ourselves has died, it can feel like the world has stopped turning. We can feel as if our lives will never be the same, because the people we love, are no longer a part of it.

The residual effect of any loss is grief.

It doesn't matter what the circumstances are (i.e., a person in active addiction, family difficulties, or even romantic break-ups), it puts undue strain on the heart. Why? Because we know what it means to have loved so deeply, and now we've been left with a void to fill.

Any of these situations can throw you into a tailspin as we mourn those who are no longer a part of our own lives. Addiction is a form of death. As the addict dies before the eyes of their family, a part of each family member dies along with them.

The question is, how long do we allow grief to stick around?

The answer is different for everyone who has lost someone they love. For me, my sorrowful heart has walked the path of grief many times. There are those who have crossed the Great Divide due to their addiction. Although I know we shall meet again one day, not having them in the physical world has been devastating. There are also many people still living who I have loved deeply yet are no longer a part of my life. They say, "Time heals all wounds," yet grief has certainly been my companion as I walk this long and winding road toward better days.

In every situation, prayer is the one thing that got me through. Prayer can be as formal or as informal as you would like it to be. It is a way to commune with a Higher Power and create a pathway for your grief to be released. Through prayer, we can ask for those we've lost, living and dead, to receive our love in absentia. We can also pray to find a peaceful resolution within ourselves as well.

Author's Reflections

Who are you grieving currently? This applies to both the living and the dearly departed. Grief applies on all fronts here.

Who is the addict who's still living, that you may feel the need to wish well, yet wish away for now?

This is also a great time to remember those who have already passed due to their addiction, and begin to heal the wound left behind by them.

Were you able to share words of peace before their passing, or do you feel burdened by hate, regret, or remorse?

What is your addict's name? It is healing to write it down and to remember who they were, or are. This is another opportunity for you to make a journal entry.

Revisit my prayer page during this time and say a prayer for the addict in need, living or passed. It will not only elevate their soul, but yours as well.

MEMOIR OF THE DIARIST

Journal your thoughts in the space below.

THE OUTSIDE OBSERVER

Like the addict, the outside observer comes in many shapes and sizes, but all have one thing in common. They are each connected by the thread of addiction, and that thread is their love for an addict. Each family is fighting a similar battle, although the external circumstances may look very different.

Each experience is layered and fought, to varying degrees within the outside observer's everyday life. This battle may have been going on for months, years, or generations. Regardless, if you look closely enough, you will see how the battles essence is influencing the outside observer's ability to lead a normal life.

On the surface, everything may appear to be fine. This is due in part to the outside observer's ability to adapt and act "normally." However, it is a juggling act, and like the clown in the circus tent, the Dragon becomes the ringmaster. Each person is simply dancing to his tune. When a plate is dropped and broken, the circus clown continues on as if nothing has even happened. They just add a fresh plate to their act, and move forward in the illusion of a balanced life.

Who are these jugglers that have become so adept at the game? You probably know, because you're probably one of them. They are the mothers, fathers, spouses, siblings, friends, and extended family of an addict. One of them may even be the addict's closest confidant. This would be the person they turn to when knee-deep in the muck and the mire of addiction.

"Enabler" is a word that comes to mind in this instance. It is often used to describe the outside observer, and one that strikes at the hearts of many. Why? Because love is so very present during this time. When you can only see the love you have for your addict, you may not even realize the damage enabling can do. This behavior needs to be looked at with an open mind to see the truth of your own actions. It is the only way you can be liberated from this dynamic.

Remember the God-given gift of free will that I spoke about earlier? Just like our addict, we have it as well. Ask yourselves this: are you using it as a way to cope, or is the Dragon influencing you to use this gift when it comes to enabling?

Manipulation is a powerful motivator, and this can be easy to forget, given all we have to fear. Sometimes we must choose what's good for ourselves, yet it doesn't mean we do not care about our addict.

There are so many forms of addictions and drugs to talk about: alcohol, pills, benzos, heroin, crack, cocaine, and meth, the list goes on. And let's not forget about the silent killer on the street: fentanyl. Remember, addiction does not discriminate and can swallow a family whole.

As an outside observer, I have seen addiction happening to multiple members of my family and close friends. Each choosing a different drug of choice, which can make life hard to navigate at times. You must know what the drug of choice is for the addict and move forward from there. All drug use will cause erratic behavior, and it may be more amplified depending on what drug they are using. No matter what they choose to use, they will all turn into some form of the Dragon.

This is where knowledge becomes power for the outside observer.

The savior complex is real!!!!

Outside observers come up with all kinds of tactics that they think will get their addict clean and sober. They range from locking them in a room, forcing them into a rehab, and even following them 24/7. None of these options are viable, but in those moments of desperation they are certainly tempting.

From my years of personal experience, I can say that all addicts do need to work some form of a program, one that serves them in an uplifting way. The problem with an addict is that they are lazy. They only want the easy fix, and they don't want to do the work involved to get sober. The Dragon has created such a sophisticated game that the addict thinks they only need that drug to be happy.

The number-one thing an addict needs to move toward sobriety is inner strength supported by God. I know some of you may have a different perspective, but for those I've known who have recovered, God was a big part of that recovery.

I will share a bit of my story now. It concerns just one drug, heroin, which seems to be a big one for many of my close friends and family, but again, it applies to all, so let's start there.

Heroin is cheap and easier than you might think to get on the streets. It is also highly addictive. When kids become addicted, they will often do anything, even sell their own bodies, for a bag of dope. That is the hardcore reality, and one that is not easy to accept. There are even websites where girls and boys can go to offer themselves up for sex so they can get money to support their habit. Some of the dealers will even pimp them out and pay them in dope. What a sickening game the Dragon has created.

For many years, I saw addiction in extended family members before it hit my own home. I watched, and perhaps judged a bit, because I did not have a full understanding of how addiction worked. It wasn't until it landed on my own doorstep, that reality slapped me in the face.

When I first started seeing it in someone who was very close to me, I went into a state of denial. Fifteen years old is way too young for anyone to use heroin, or any drug for that matter. Shocked and with no idea what the signs were, I went in with blinders on. I believed that I was going to save my addict because I knew their heart. This one, I thought, is different from the rest. If my influence could reach my addict as a child, surely it was strong enough to penetrate the haze of drug use. This was when the wild ride began, along with my crash course on addiction and the brain.

The first signs were physical sickness. I heard the excuses "I have the flu," or "I am just tired," followed by shouts to "Stop bugging me!" I loved my addict so much that I pushed my intuitive nudges aside and allowed the haze of deceit to cloud my judgment. I placated my addict and avoided the truth that was staring me right in the face!

When I found out it was a twenty-five-year-old man who pulled my fifteen-year-old into the world of hardcore drugs, the range of emotions were wild. From anger to tears, panic to determination, I was willing to do anything to help. Looking back at those particular moments, I didn't realize that I had been rendered helpless. The Dragon had already made himself at home in my addict.

There are undeniable signs that someone is using heroin. I will list a few here that I have witnessed. Some of these signs can also point to other drug use as well.

- Lying
- Getting into trouble
- Argumentative
- Lacking in personal hygiene
- Sudden changes in personality
- Increased sleeping
- Acne
- Itchy skin
- Runny nose from snorting (which is what my addict does; others have bruising from shooting up.)
- Scabs on the skin
- Nodding out
- Puking
- Strange body movements

- Pinpoint pupils

Even when the drug use was confirmed, I still tried to look the other way. It was painful to see my addict like that, and I wanted to fix them. I didn't fully realize that I couldn't. It really became apparent when my addict said to me, "I like being high and I have no intention of stopping."

My addict was in and out of court-appointed recovery as a minor, and upon coming out, would immediately use. I will share how I feel about rehabs later. Again, my addict told me, "I only went to rehab because I had to go. I like being high; let me be great."

Ten years and countless invaluable lessons later, I can state with the utmost certainty that there is no timetable when it comes to recovery. We simply continue to pray that the addict will make that choice one day.

Until then, each person will remain an outside observer, wringing their hands in times of strife and clinging to those fleeting moments of joy when the addict asks us for our help.

This is when we begin to believe that it is finally over! But alas, the addict and their addiction are two very big beasts who leave a burden for the outside observer to bear. When your loved one is an addict, you know this cycle all too well. This is when you must be honest with yourselves. You must begin to recognize it is not your battle to fight and win. It is theirs.

My advice moving forward is so simple and yet so difficult all at the same time. While you are still hoping and praying for recovery, you must find a way to make peace with their addiction. It doesn't mean you have to close the door to them, unless that's the best option for you. Only you know the answer to this.

For me, and what I have shared with other mothers of addicts, is this: if you can, grieve them now. Make peace with their eventual death so you are not completely crushed if and when that day comes. Any person using drugs is playing with fire; that's the reality. When you can make peace with their addiction and the potential consequences, you can free yourself from their drama.

In my home, my addict knows that I do not want to see them high. I told them, "If you are using, don't come around." I still get a mixed bag, and I treasure the sober moments when lasting memories are made. These are the bright spots, and when I get to see the person who has emerged from under the Dragon's shadow. This is where I gain a new sense of who they are, and who they were meant to be.

People, especially those working in rehab centers, will tell you that it's an addict's job to relapse. I disagree. If we put that out there and the addict adopts this theory, then relapses will always be in their future. This is part of what rehab centers teach addicts in their 28-day programs. This is why rehabilitation requires a facelift, in my opinion.

The old days and ways need to change, starting with:

1. End the one-size-fits-all philosophy. Take the time to get to the bottom of the addict's wound. They are all individuals with different lives.

2. Stop making recovery financially inaccessible. Most people do not have $40,000 to invest in a treatment program.

3. Realize that an addict needs longer than 28 days to heal.

4. Stop prescribing meds to an addict in recovery. In most cases, the chances of the addict finding a doctor on the outside to continue their regimen are slim to none. They should be weaned from all drugs and truly made sober.

5. Stop shaming the addict in circle and meetings. This is senseless and reinforces why they may have started using to begin with.

6. Figure out what works for each addict and reinforce it.

7. Give them the resources to support their recovery once they are out of rehab.

Some suggestions:

1. Have a person dedicated to following up with the addict once released.

2. Help each addict uncover their skillset, and support that. If they do not have a skillset, support them in figuring out what they want to do and offer resources (i.e., classes or apprenticeships) for their development.

3. Make sure people running meetings are truly sober.

4. Provide a true connection with businesses that will give an addict a shot at a future.

5. Utilize technology, such as virtual meetings, as this is the future for people in recovery.

6. Pair the addicts with sponsors who have knowledge of their particular drug of choice before they exit the program.

Rehabilitation facilities cannot continue to treat drug addiction with prescription drugs. Historically, this has been the go-to treatment, which only places a band-aid on the situation. If an addict is prone to laziness, what makes these centers think that the addict will find a doctor on the outside and continue with their regimen? Therapy is the best option in the end. By helping an addict face what has driven them to use in the first place, they can begin their journey toward sobriety. This is where and when the real work begins. This is where the addict can begin to heal from the inside out, drug-free.

Helping the addict reconnect to their Divine light is also very important. They were born for a purpose. They got derailed along the way. There is no such thing as a lost cause. Yes, some addicts have underlying mental health problems, and if so, they should be treated accordingly. But this doesn't mean you treat every patient with the same therapy. The addict is looking for real help, and help that is personal to them.

Along with my addict, I have seen the inner workings of these centers and the people who work there. Some of the workers inside these facilities seem to be void of compassion. I have seen their complacency as they shuffle each addict to the door at the end of the 28 days, seemingly, and without a care in the world about what will happen on the other side. If we don't change what is happening inside rehabilitation facilities, then the addict will continue to enter through a revolving door.

For a moment, stop and reflect on yourself as an outside observer. Look at the drug of choice, the treatment, and where your addict is at today. Write your thoughts in your journal and allow the wisdom of God's influence to pour from pen to paper. You will be surprised how healing and revealing the journaling process will be for you.

In closing, I know that I will never abandon ship completely, and if you're reading this book, I know that I am in good company. Your job moving forward is to find calm seas to float upon as you watch the storm from a distance. This can be the scariest place for the outside observer. It's where you surrender and have given it to God while allowing the addict the freedom of choice. The addict will choose life, continued servitude to the Dragon, or even death. This does not negate the love you have for them at any given moment. It just reinforces the love you have for yourselves.

MEMOIR OF THE DIARIST

Journal your thoughts in the space below.

A SPIRITUAL VIEW ON OPIOID ADDICTION

This subject is of real significance to me. I personally know so many people today who are struggling with addiction to opioids and street heroin. I have family members and friends who have passed away from an overdose, and others who are in the thick of it. These addicts all felt, or feel the same, as if there is no hope for the future.

The real crime is that opioid addiction and drug use is a plague, one of many that have decimated countless families across America.

It's a parent or family member's worst nightmare to find out that someone that they love is in active addiction. When this first comes to light, the outside observer still believes that the addict can be reached, only to find out it has been happening longer than they could have ever imagined. Feelings of hopelessness overtake them as they try to do the work for the addict, only to recognize that the addict is going along with it just to keep the nagging at bay. Slowly, but surely, the outside observer realizes that this fight is bigger than any they have fought in this lifetime.

Unfortunately, the fight can go on for years, filled with turmoil and fleeting moments of hope.

Over the years, some mothers have said to me, "I am so afraid that I will have to bury my child, and the thought of this is so unbearable to me."

This tugged at my heartstrings, because I recognized the feeling within myself. The way I moved through it was to prepare myself for my addict's eventual death. I forced myself to lean into "the unthinkable" so it wouldn't be such a shock if it did occur. It wasn't because my love for them had waned. It was because I realized that their addiction was consuming every free moment of my life.

In November 2016, I went to see a young lady, a heroin addict in my family. I had no idea what it was like to have an addiction to heroin or opioids and was in search of understanding.

"Why," I asked her, "do you guys use heroin?"

"Because you don't feel the pain inside of you when you are high," she replied without hesitation. "Nothing else matters. That's why we go back to it, because it makes the struggles in life more manageable. We just don't seem to care about the secrets we carry inside of us any longer."

Her response was from the most honest place within her; however, though I listened carefully, I was still not fully understanding heroin's draw. It made me begin to think, how many other addicts feel the same as she does?

That evening, I prayed to God to help me understand what she had described. I needed to know because I needed to understand how to help my own addict. I also needed to understand so I could help myself.

I had no idea that what I had asked Him to reveal to me was just around the corner...

Interestingly enough, I was scheduled to have a discogram for my back the following week. It's a very painful procedure, for which I would have to be awake, and the human side of me was fearful. When I received the prescription for Diazepam, I was told that it would take the edge off. I was relieved but had no idea that this drug was a prescription opioid.

As this drug began to kick in, all of my inhibitions were lowered, my fear and worry no longer an issue. I cared about nothing more than the feeling of this enveloping euphoria. Nothing external mattered to me at all, not even the needle being put into my spine.

I was able to lie there, even in excruciating pain, and describe in full detail what I was feeling. Yet I never flinched, not once. On the ride home, my father-in-law was chatting with me. I remember staring out the window, watching the world go by. His words seem to be strung together. They went in one ear and out the other. All I could do was nod, secretly wishing for silence, as the scenes outside moved in slow motion. This high remained with me for the remainder of the day.

The next morning, as I became sober from my high, I said to myself, now I get it. Now I understand the allure of this masterful and abusive partner in life. Never had I imagined that a drug could make you feel nothing, and joyful, all at the same time. How a drug could tune out the world around you while allowing you to view it through a different lens. Finally, I understood why people would want to chase a drug that gave them such a sense of peace in what they saw as a chaotic life.

I was so grateful to God for granting my request, and in full living color. He had given me a view into the addict's experience so I could fully understand what is happening with these addicts and on a soul level no less. I became aware of how addiction to heroin is such an easy pit to fall into, and such a hard one to climb out of. This pit is where the Dragon is waiting, and where the addict becomes a prisoner to his wicked ways.

You see, when a person uses heroin, they become a shadow of their former self. The truth of who they are no longer matters to them. To work toward something productive in life becomes an afterthought. The easy road is the one they choose to travel because the road to recovery forces them to face reality. The euphoria of heroin is so powerful that they are taken to a place that has no reality, yet it is very real to the addict. Why? Because it does not compute in their brains.

We all know that an addict will lie, steal, and even exchange sexual favors for a high. They will abandon all logic because they just want to feel good, even if only for a moment. As soon as that moment wears off, they long for more. The cravings kick in, and they are off to the races. They will do anything to get back to that feeling of not feeling anymore.

This is why "tough love" does not work. When they are high and void of feeling, they don't even acknowledge consequences, let alone care about them. The euphoria of heroin is so powerful that the love they are seeking is in a powder form.

I know so many kids who are in active addiction today. I also know many of their parents. They feel helpless because they cannot save their addict from themselves. Unless you have walked a mile in a parent's shoes, you will never know the depth of their pain, and at times, the shame that is felt.

Through my own perspective, I began to understand what was happening, but it didn't make it less painful to watch. Here are a few of my thoughts.

We never truly know what an addict is going through. Were they a victim of sexual abuse as a child, or perhaps had an absentee parent? Could they be struggling to fit in or are they being bullied at school? Maybe they have fallen in with the wrong crowd or introduced to heroin by someone they know and trust. They could even have a chemical imbalance in the brain that was never addressed.

The sad reality is this: when the addiction makes its presence known, they are labeled as "junkies." Such a damaging and ugly word.

I do know this much: if we do not get to the root cause within the addict, they will continue to dance with the Dragon for a lifetime, as drugs have become their only friend and lover.

Recovery is the only option. Yet, if they haven't hit their rock bottom, they may be in denial that they need help at all. Rehab is only one part of the deal. For those who have never done drugs, understand that the cravings from certain drugs can last for years. Getting past those cravings is the first big step. Releasing the people, the places, and the things that connect an addict to heroin (or any drug) goes right along with it. (Re)learning self-worth and how to love themselves sober is another step. Unburying the pain of why they use is most important. Inviting God in, and asking Him for mercy and healing is what makes recovery possible.

Now, I want to discuss how technology, specifically social media, has become the Dragon's partner in crime and one of the addict's biggest obstacles. This digital super highway has empowered the Dragon and changed the dynamics of the game, one click at a time.

All they have to do is get online and find a hookup. It is like an addict's "Door Dash," where any drug you desire is on a menu and ready to be ordered. How can the addict truly heal when the Dragon is beckoning them from the phone in their pocket?

My advice to everyone reading this: don't ask someone why is your kid using. Every addict and family has a backstory. Ask, "What can I do to help you through this difficult time?" Stop judging the addict or their family members. Try to speak to them with kindness, because you will never be able to fully step into their shoes. Start speaking to them with honesty and understanding, even if that means telling them that you don't understand. Words are powerful. They can either wound a person or elevate them to new heights. Be mindful that you will never really know how damaging the stigma of drug addiction is to their spirit.

This is a fight that only the addict can beat. Praying for them is the only thing that you can control!!!!

We do not live in a perfect world, but even the most impossible feats can be accomplished with the right intent behind them.

UTILIZING THE
POWER OF LOVE

*E*veryone reading this may be saying to themselves, "Yes, I get it, but now what? How do I move forward without feeling as if I have abandoned my addict?"

Let's talk about Love, shall we?

We will each love another in our own way, based on how we were taught to love and be loved as children. This is the wisdom of love's vibration. Yet, with every vibration there is an opposite dynamic.

Love is the opposite of hate. Hate connects us to anger, and it is anger that keeps hate alive. All outside observers of an addict go through a range of emotions, and rightfully so. Why? Because we are also entangled in this web of deceit. Our hands, our hearts, and our desire to fix them is what keeps us connected to our addict through loves influence.

I have heard many different theories about how to move forward. One is tough love. As we discussed previously, when an addict is using, they only care about being high in that moment.

Even with tough love, they will still move on to their next fix.

Why? Because your tough love means nothing to them. Pay attention here, because this is where the addict becomes masterful at manipulation.

They will seem to become compliant; they will work at convincing you that they are ready to get help. They will be all too willing to tolerate what they see as your nagging, for the instant gratification they are looking for. This is where they will be in complete agreement, with their hands out, saying, "I just need this one thing from you now. Tomorrow I will go to detox." If the word "tomorrow" is part of the equation of their compliance, you must recognize that tomorrow will never happen.

This is when you must take control of the situation. It is when you will utter one word. If you do, one of two things will happen: the addict will begin bartering with you, or out the door they will go.

The secret word is NO!!!

NO is your superpower. It can be very difficult for most of us to say. But once you get strong in your NO, you gain strength in your position.

One thing you must be aware of, is that your NO may result in trouble for the addict. You will have no control over the situation. You just have to find peace in your decision. Easier said than done, I know. When you're in doubt try to remember that the addict's free will, is leading the charge.

The truth of the matter is this: if you cannot, or are unwilling to understand the power of saying NO, the cycle of stagnation will continue.

Standing in your NO allows you to start building a new foundation. It is a foundation built not only on love for them, but for yourself as well.

When Love gets propped up in this unique way, it allows you to rebuild and update what is broken. Your new super-power is connected to your old foundation, but with updates to support you now.

Love's Wisdom

Please be mindful of this, that what you teach to your own children today will become the foundation on which they will teach their own in the future.

Plant the seeds of love within their hearts now, and they will surely know peace for a lifetime.

It is through your own understanding where you must apply these principles.

It is from here and where each child must be given order and discipline to learn from, yet it must be built upon a foundation of love.

For if it is not built upon love, then that foundation will surely crumble beneath their feet

Channeled August 22, 2013

Author's Reflections

As I leave you with this beautiful, channeled wisdom, it becomes the teacher for you, and about your own foundation. It gives you a pathway toward understanding how to support yourself as your loved one is in active addiction.

If applied, it can show you where your foundation has been crumbling beneath your family's feet. It can guide you in understanding where you can begin to repair that foundation and restore it to its former glory. Or maybe even replace the crumbling part of it with something new.

Let's get those journals out. Reflect on what has been written and the wisdom shared. What comes to mind?

The key to learning here is to be honest about the love given and received. The order and discipline your foundation is built upon, and from where your love is doled out. Is it conditional or unconditional? Write down your thoughts and move on.

MEMOIR OF THE DIARIST

Journal your thoughts in the space below.

EVOLVING THROUGH PAIN

It is through the difficult choices that you grow.

Through the pain that you are healed.

*Through the heart where you learn acceptance
and more.*

*If you can see yourselves as only a part of the bigger
picture, then maybe you could move through all
things in life.*

Movement through grace.

Gentleness toward self and others.

Taking stock of your own part in the process of living.

*Day by day, week by week, year by year, you evolve
and grow due to your own experiences.*

*Moving forward, be grateful each day for every
moment of your life.*

Cherish the people within it.

Be delivered to the doorway of transformation.

Inspired Writing October 11, 2017

Author's Reflections

Life with an addict can be a never-ending roller coaster of chaos, and one we desperately want to get off of.

The way to exit the ride is through the wisdom written. The opportunity for understanding resides in the words above.

Take a moment and allow your own voice to be heard. Put pen to paper and insert yourself in the midst of the writing. Find a way to move through your pain and to the doorway of transformation.

It is worth the journey toward healing the broken pieces of today, while leaving the rubble behind. When you do this, you will see clearly the pathway that awaits you.

MEMOIR OF THE DIARIST

Journal your thoughts in the space below.

A SPIRITUAL PERSPECTIVE
OF THE OUTSIDE OBSERVER

As I sit here and ponder the world around me, I can sense where I too have been thrown off balance.

The he said/she said/they said can get the best of any person. The opinions of one go against the grain of another. Confusion exploding in the midst of a crisis.

Common sense falling on Deaf Ears.

In the addict's eyes, the right to choose for themselves feels as if it has gone out the window. The shaming from the outside observer, who wants to choose for them, becomes abrasive. It triggers their feelings of powerlessness. This is when the addict stands their ground and negotiations of any kind are stalled.

It is now the addict versus the outside observer, and what it means for both sides to be in the pit of active addiction. The pain for both sides becomes the middleman.

This is heavy stuff, and people from every corner of the world are in the mix. With such a heavy load to bear, some just feel like giving up.

You may be wondering when it will all end.

How do we correct the course we have been traveling on?

It seems as if we have forgotten to take the time to float within the "Zone" of our spirituality so that we can connect to our own truth. This is where we have been allowing others to tell us whether we are right or wrong, and where we have become so quick to anger.

Ultimately, how can we disconnect ourselves from this energy to see the bigger picture?

For 26 years, I had an amazing spiritual teacher named Miss Jackie. I sat within her circle, enveloped in her wisdom and guidance. Miss Jackie taught me how to tap into my own spirituality. These tools were her gift to me, yet I have forgotten at times, to tap in when I am immersed in the midst of active addiction. As I ponder this, I can hear her words clearly in my head:

> *When the grain of another person's beliefs begins to push you around, it is your job to move away from the fray.*
>
> *Each person has a truth deep within them. It is not anyone's (i.e., the addict's) job to convince you otherwise.*
>
> *Remember this, it is their perfect problem to deal with and not yours.*
>
> *You each have something of value to learn from the path that you are traveling now. It is up to you to discern this truth for yourself and move on accordingly.*

Miss Jackie would then wink and chuckle from the other side of the table.

I can still feel her sweet presence beside me. It is like sitting for a reading with her today. I can feel her words resonating deeply with my own truth. The reminder is that there are many paths to follow, and it is my choice as to where I place my own two feet.

Never forget the elders who came before you.

Those who have gifted you with nuggets of wisdom to carry within your hearts and minds for a lifetime.

The Teachers who have taught you how to "go within" for the answers.

This is where they have shown you that the outside world is an exterior expression of multiple opinions.

Channeled August 18, 2021

Your truth, their truth, and the creation of the pathways that those in power want you to follow. This is where the Dragon has chosen his field, to battle upon with you, but only if you allow him to.

I am here to remind you about free will. It is by choice whether you jump into the fray or sit this one out. It does not mean that you should not stand for something. It just means that you should not allow yourselves to be drawn into an internal battle with your own beliefs.

There it is. The battle within you. The hard truth that becomes a pill too big to swallow. Ignoring what your own inner voice is screaming from within, as you render yourselves helpless. But are you?

Never allow the addict to quiet your own intuitive voice of reason. This is where you must also allow your addict the same freedoms. This is a tricky path to follow as your own truth begs to be heard! Yet the group of souls locked into one side (addiction) or the other (outside observer) have something of value to gain from the ugly experience of active addiction.

Sometimes, the only thing you can do is love them from a distance. The other choice would be to invite their chaos to wreak havoc within your own home and lives. Knowing this is one thing; making the tough decision is another, but a line in the sand must be drawn to change the dynamics of the Dragon's game.

Hard as it may be, if you find yourselves drawn to speak out, do so from a place of peace within you. This is where you can offer up an opinion without the need to change the course of another person's lesson to learn. The lesson for the outside observer is learning how to peacefully coexist within a world of many, while dealing with an addict.

Balance is key.

FINDING YOUR BALANCE

*Life is full of so many different emotions, that is why
it is called the human experience.*

*You see dear ones, on the opposite side of the veil you
will know only love. This is because that is the vibration of the spirit world, and your soul is created and
born of this energy.*

*Now, on the Earth plane your ego has a hand in
creating your reality. This is where the emotions come
into play and where balance is lost.*

*As you go about your earthly incarnation, the choice is
yours on how you choose to live it.*

*If you will, recognize where your emotions have
helped to create your current set of circumstances.*

*A small shift in perception, can and will, create a
formal change in your own reality.*

Channeled August 17, 2014

*O*ur lives are both simple and complex; yet, it may seem that the complexities can far outweigh the simplicity of life, as we try to achieve that perfect balance. This is especially true when we are dealing with an addict and their addiction.

Each of us were born into this lifetime and this physical existence by choice. From our physical bodies to our current set of circumstances, they were all pre-planned by our soul for lessons and growth.

Nothing happens by accident or chance; everything good, bad or indifferent is for our greatest good and highest joy.

Now, this may not sound so good if you are struggling with an addict. If only you could see the flipside of the coin!

Struggles can be overcome; you do have the free will to tap into that strength. You may just have to dig a little bit deeper and remember that your soul was, and is, prepared for this exact moment in time.

Your emotions are a force of nature!!!

Every person born will experience the good, the bad, and neutral. The key is in remembering that how you experience any of the above involves your emotional state of being.

Your emotions are a big part of the equation when dealing with addiction. Some humans allow their emotions to rule the day. This is when you can become a prisoner, a dangerous perspective to be stuck within when dealing with an addict. The key is finding balance between the positive and the negative emotions. Love and hate are great examples of this. We love our addict, but we hate their addiction.

No matter what I go through, I always try to remember one thing: it is up to me to change the flow of energy that I may find myself stuck within. This isn't always easy to do when dealing with an addict, so I try not to get overwhelmed and lost in my emotions. Our emotions can be extremely powerful, and this is where we tend to lose sight.

Visualize it like this: when we're enraged, we are just like a horse with blinders on, and we have no peripheral vision. We can only see what is right in front of us. The words captured in that one tiny channeled sentence below, hold great power for the outside observer.

Try to see beyond that which has consumed you, and this is where you will gain clarity.

It's an exercise worthy of your attention and can change everything when put into perspective.

Author's Reflections

The only way to break any cycle is through change. Change is created by you, the author. Remember, this is your story and edits need to be made as you are writing it.

When any change is implemented, you must remain loyal to those changes. It is easy to fall backwards because the past holds a familiar essence, and one that we tend to latch onto. It is when we untether ourselves from the old baggage that we free ourselves up to experience what the future holds.

This is where your choices begin to shift, not only the landscape, but the people around you. You are now open to become the teacher of your experiences. This is where you will find many others' standing in your former footwear and looking for guidance.

It is where you will begin to teach those same people through the actions taken by you, which have been experienced through your own journey of emotions and more.

Before you move on, make a note about what changes you could make that would benefit your life now. Remember to allow your emotional adventures to lend a hand.

MEMOIR OF THE DIARIST

Journal your thoughts in the space below.

EQUALITY VERSUS EGO

I t is written, that in the eyes of God, all people are created equal.

The addict, and the outside observer, are given equal ground to stand upon as they stand within the energy of their own truth.

This is practiced through the ego of man and where judgment casts its shadow.

It has become apparent that the physical world is out of alignment with Universal Law. One cannot be separated from the other. Universal Law will always supersede man's idea of law (i.e., the ego).

In today's world, cracks are showing, and humanity is falling within those cracks. In this case, it encompasses addiction. As the addict falls, so does the outside observer.

The old paradigm of drug addiction is twisting the truth to stay in control. It is the only way to keep the Dragon alive.

Truth is, we need to see with clarity in the midst of this chaos, or we will find ourselves in the same old boat. The Dragon will continue to find a new crew to row his boat, as the ego of man displays his arrogance.

Remember, the Dragon is the ringmaster in this circus.

This is where you will see that nothing new is truly born here as the sleight of hand becomes the blindfold over all sets of eyes.

It is all about the ego versus God's Law, and the idea of equality for all. The ego of man will never win in this instance.

Here are some questions worthy of reflection:

How do we allow the old paradigm of addiction to die a peaceful death?

How do we welcome in the new paradigm waiting to be born (sobriety), one in which all people can get behind, and what is begging to be realized (honesty and truth)?

My personal views are these:

We have a world in crisis, government structures and their officials gone rogue. Old money and the powerful who dole it out are still in charge. They try to hide behind the smokescreens that they have created, yet the cracks are far too big for them to find a safe haven any longer. Money rules the world and drugs have been one of their biggest money grabs. This is where the ego of man is on full display.

But alas, the sleeping giant has awoken, and that sleeping giant is you. It is up to you to connect the dots of the drugs on America's streets and how they got here. It is also up to you on how you choose to have your voice heard in the Dragon's forum. It is ultimately up to you to be a part of the change desired for your addict and your family.

The "War on Drugs" is real, and the real battles are happening. They are not being fought in the halls of Congress, but within the homes of families across this great land.

Spiritually, for change to take hold people must become an example of the change that they desire to see. It may be born in the NO. It may be born from unconditional love and understanding. But it most definitely is awakened from the truth that we have all been hiding from.

The truth is that we have a drug problem in America and my child, spouse, et cetera are all caught up within the ravages of addiction. There is no government body that is coming to save us or them. The fight is now our own to bear and to beat!

Addiction is an ugly pill to swallow. Yet to be swallowed up by the Dragon's influence is even more detrimental to both sides.

Finding middle ground in the energy of deceit is the only way. This is where balance is re-gained and your own truth about addiction can then be supported.

The positive will always trump the negative. But keep in mind that they are on the opposite side of the same energy. It is somewhere in the middle that the energy balances itself out, and where the world and its people can live in harmony with one another.

The harmony may be experienced with people just like yourself. After all, isn't this what the addict has already beautifully displayed? They really have been the teacher of this energy, yet the ugliness of their addiction has blinded us from learning the lesson at hand.

So, how do we move forward and create true change? Every human alive must find that middle ground for themselves and allow it room to grow. The middle ground for everyone is different, but the end result is peace for the outside observer.

What do you deem your middle ground to be? Finding understanding in your own situation is key here. What do you expect from your addict, and most importantly, yourself?

When these things are given room to breathe, it is then that the outside observer has room to implement the change needed for harmony's loving embrace.

This is where the birth of "Equality for All" is now given a platform to stand upon.

Today you are given the opportunity to find your own place within the world of addiction. This is where you have been given the roadmap toward peace, if only you allow harmony to be your guide.

Reflect on what has been written and insert yourself into the equation. Continue building on that story of yours so that you can see yourself within it. It is not only about the addict; it is also about you.

MEMOIR OF THE DIARIST

Journal your thoughts in the space below.

HOW MANY HATS DO WE WEAR IN A DAY?

We are spouses, parents, employees, homemakers, caretakers, spiritual beings, and so on. We spend most of our day doing for others as our needs become secondary at best. Most of us were taught to put our work, home, and families first to ensure a happy life.

As an outside observer, we seem to have put our addict's needs before our own, and that must change.

As our soul begins to call our name, we daydream about all the things we would love to do. However, we never make the time to do them. Our efforts to save our addict seem to have taken priority. It seems that we have lost the balance in our lives as the scales have tipped heavily to one side or the other. This is when we need to recognize how the addict has commandeered our time.

Every person wants a healthy, happy, and peaceful life, but some of us just don't know where to begin. Well, the good news is that today is that day! If you are willing, you can begin to find that peaceful, easy feeling once again. The key is, you must be willing to do the work and nurture yourself just as you have nurtured your addict.

It really is not that difficult. It is just putting down the guilt and recognizing the need for balance in your life. This is where you allow yourself to reclaim it. You can take baby steps or jump right in as you adjust the scales to make time for yourself.

There are far too many souls lost to addiction in this physical world. And there are those of us who have given them an endless lifeline. Each of us is waiting on the shoreline, hoping our addicts survive the riptide. The thing about lifelines is this: Who is holding yours?

The problem, as I see it, is the addict has become completely consumed with selfishness and void of selflessness. It is an imbalance of energy and where manipulation is easily achieved. This is where you can cut the cord that tethers you to them, and see this truth for yourselves. You are more than just a means to an end for your addict. You also deserve to be selfish at this moment, while remaining guilt-free as you make this choice.

Never forget that you are a beautiful being of light, a soul living in a human existence yet fulfilling soul contracts on many fronts. The thing about the outside observer is this: they have forgotten that they have a bigger purpose in life. Once you realize this simple truth, freedom washes over you.

You were not born solely to be a savior to your addict while they continue to dance with the Dragon. Finding your way out of the addict's darkness is the gift to the outside observer.

There is no time like the present to remember those purposeful moments in life that have yet to be fulfilled. The cool thing about the soul is that it waits patiently for you to return to center. It gives you an opportunity to remember the whys of your existence. It's a great time to revisit what you wanted to be when you grew up. This is where you can revisit the past briefly. You can then activate the light of who you are and who you were meant to be.

Begin with a simple reflection of gratitude, for example, sitting with a cup of coffee and reflecting on the beauty of the day before you. You can utilize the sound of silence or the beauty of music during these moments. By allowing your soul's wisdom to present itself during this time, and writing down your daily thoughts, you begin to move in ways that serve you now. This is where you can re-establish a rapport with self!!!

The only way out of the darkness is to pursue the light!!!

This is a brand-new hat that you can add to your collection and begin to wear with pride.

Author's Reflections

In closing, I want to share some words of wisdom.

You cannot change the past nor worry about the future.

The only control that you have is to be fully present for yourself, at this moment.

This is where you allow life to unfold in a way that serves your highest good and greatest joy today.

Never forget that it is okay to be happy. Give yourself permission to experience what God has intended for you. This way, you don't miss out on those tiny moments that will shape your life moving forward.

Write down one thing that would bring you great joy today. Try not to make it about your addict. Make it about you.

MEMOIR OF THE DIARIST

Journal your thoughts in the space below.

THE LIGHT AFTER THE STORM

There is always a light after any storm in life and in nature.

There must be, otherwise, how could we ever find our way out of the darkness?

Each of us were promised a sunrise and a sunset at the beginning and at the end of each day lived.

The duality of one aspect that signifies life and death, new and old, present and past.

The sunrise signifies new beginnings, birth, and renewal. This is the time when the awakening occurs within.

The sunset signifies endings, a mark in time, the past. This is where we are allowed to let go of what has already occurred.

As you begin this new day, you are asked to find gratitude for what the day has to offer.

*This is where you are allowed to let go of your yester-
day and where you can say thank you for today.*

This is what it means to live in the present moment.

*What it shows you is that life is liquid, time is pre-
cious, and when wasted it is squandered.*

Say thank you out loud.

*Acknowledge your gratitude for allowing you to
recognize the importance of not being held captive by
the past.*

*Allow yourself to see what serves your greatest good
and highest joy in this moment.*

*Ask for the grace of strength so that you can embrace
this truth.*

Channeled and Inspired Writing January 19, 2019

Author's Reflection

*The parable above gives you an opportunity to reflect on the
past and be mindful of your present moment in time. It has so
much wisdom intertwined within the writing. This is where
you will gain a fresh perspective of where you find yourself at,
in the Dragon's game.*

*The key is this: You can leave the game anytime you are ready
to. The reason you stay is out of fear of the unknown. You are
used to cleaning up the damage that the storm has left behind.*

This is a boardgame with many moves.

The addict in the game has been hoarding the dice, because if they roll them, they will have to make a move. When they are ready for a change in scenery, they will most likely roll the dice. The fear for you, the outside observer, is that you have no control over what they will roll the dice for.

You have to realize that the storm damage left behind is for them to clean up. That is the hard reality for the outside observer to understand, yet a very real part of the Dragon's game.

Ask yourself this: why is it so hard to allow my addict to do for themselves? Why am I always picking up the pieces?

Honesty matters; write it down and move on.

MEMOIR OF THE DIARIST

Journal your thoughts in the space below.

MEETINGS

*R*eflections of the past.

Disclaimer: As we move forward, I want you to under-
stand this: when I talk about leaders who are former
addicts, and from my own experience with them, most
of them have not yet crossed the threshold of being healed
themselves, and they falter. This is where they wear
two masks: one of the meeting's leader; the other of the
addict. To truly help another in their journey of recov-
ery, a person must be fully recovered themselves and teach
from that place of addiction. If they haven't, then no one
benefits from their council. This is when meetings do not
benefit the addict or the outside observer in search of help.

There was a time in my life when I didn't know where
to turn. I was guided by a friend to attend a support meeting
with my addict. I was so ready to do whatever it took and was
onboard for the long haul. So off we went, attending a handful
of meetings together, always with the same outcome. In fact, I
began to question why these meetings even existed.

The meetings in my area were led by a man who was very
popular in Illinois. His M.O. was always the same. During his
opening, he would present as a man filled with compassion

and understanding. He made people feel comfortable and gave them a false sense of hope. He encouraged people to take their guard down. What he was really doing was preparing to go in for the kill.

After a bit of evangelism, during which he demonstrated his skill as a public speaker, he would seek out the newest addict in the room. After he made them feel comfortable, he would start asking for people to share their stories of addiction. His spiel went something like this.

"Raise your hand," he said, "and share your story. Tell us your drug of choice and why you use. Your story will help others in the room."

People who had been around this man for a while began sharing their stories.

Some were still struggling, while others went on to tell their story of recovery. From my perspective, all of the stories shared a thread of truth, one that would connect them to the new addicts in the room. I listened as these people spoke. The evangelist supported them, giving them words of encouragement. Little did I know that some of these people were a part of his inner circle.

By this time, the new addicts in the room thought it was safe to share. That's when the truth of the man behind the pious façade emerged. I watched, horrified, as he approached them and began screaming in their faces. It was like attending a talk show, where juvenile delinquents are taken to task. They were being scolded, shamed, and humiliated in front of the audience as if that would break them of their bad behavior. It was very unsettling to witness. I watched in horror as the addict was made to feel useless in front of a group of total strangers. In fact, it perpetuated the problem and helped no one. The already fractured spirit of the addict was further broken.

I sat in silence and watched as the addicts, including my own, walked out of the meeting and straight back to using. They did this as a way to bury the pain of being humiliated.

Why, I thought to myself, *why is this even being supported?*

Mercifully, the man said he needed a cigarette break. He gathered outside with the addicts from the group who were looking for guidance. All of them standing in a circle, like a group of lifelong friends, chatting and laughing, exposing the charade. The only ones who were not gathered in that circle were the new addicts. They were now busy finding a hook-up in the parking lot, and back to the Dragon they went.

The truth came to light months later. The man, the evangelist, was secretly using. He ended up dying from a drug overdose.

My observations were these: The evangelist had been chosen by a former addict to run the outreach program in my county. He was celebrated by so many and even had a popular podcast. This same man began to set the standard for the meetings that he was in charge of running. He was even bold enough to place his addict friends as meeting leaders, and where they perpetuated the same toxic dynamic.

In my opinion, he did nothing positive for the community. He was a slick talker, had a lot of charisma, and people were drawn to him, kind of like the wily character the addict presents when using. I could see exactly how he hid his drug use by the way he bullied other addicts. He said it was all in the name of making them honest about their addiction, while all the while he was hiding his own. He was masterful at manipulation.

Sharing this with you brings up old feelings of pain for me, along with the defeat and discomfort that my addict and I felt during those meetings.

The clique mentality within these meetings was like sitting with an abusive partner. Addicts, while in active addiction, were encouraged to shame the new addicts in the group, who, of course, had no idea what was going on. These addicts who were actively using, shared a common bond: they wanted to hold a person back from truly recovering, just like them. These meetings were not a gateway toward healing. They were, in fact, a backdoor to the Dragon's den of using.

Those meetings, for my addict, only perpetuated the belief that there was no life beyond a bag of dope.

I, who was there to support my addict, was told by the group leader to just be quiet and listen. I was told this is what the addicts need. It was not easy to stay silent in the face of this bullying, which I would never condone in a sober setting, let alone this one. I couldn't believe that these supposedly "former" addicts were so void of compassion, so aggressive, and cruel to people looking for support.

It never occurred to me that the leaders of the meetings still had things to work out for themselves. They claimed sobriety as a badge of honor, yet sobriety was a far reality for the leader of this group. I later learned he wasn't the only one secretly using.

These people were nothing more than an example of deceit. They all elevated themselves to a place of power, even though they were powerless over their own addiction.

It is a vicious cycle and one that needs to be broken.

There are many things you can do moving forward. One of them, despite what I just shared with you, is attending meetings. There are two types of meetings. One where you and your addict go together, and the other is like a support group for the person of an addict, you, the outside observer.

I have only attended meetings with my addict while they were in active addiction or recovery. The other type, I have heard good things about but cannot make a recommendation because I have not experienced one.

Support groups are like fellowship at a church. Some people really thrive in the environment and do well mentally, physically, and emotionally because of them. The people who gain much out of these meetings are the ones who participate. Sharing their experiences with others can open the doorway of healing for themselves.

In my experience, there are great leaders, and others who fall far short of greatness. If you personally have gained something from the meetings you are attending, I suggest that you stay the course. Again, while meetings are not for everyone, some do thrive in that environment.

The keys to success are these: ask yourself, what are you taking home from the group setting to work with on your own. It is important to carry the principles and philosophies that are shared beyond the group meeting and apply them in real time. This way, you will be growing, rather than staying on the hamster wheel of stagnation.

Let's also talk about the conventional ways of dealing with your loved one's active addiction through meetings. These would be called recovery meetings. These meetings usually occur when your addict is participating in an inpatient program. The addict's family members are encouraged to attend along with their addict. It is one avenue created where resources are provided so you can understand the interpersonal dynamics caused by active addiction. These meetings not only provide support and resources for those in active addiction, they also give a window of understanding about the powerful draw to their drug of choice.

I personally don't care for support meetings. Why? Because my experience in all of them has been the same: talking, sharing, and shaming the addict. For me, it all comes back to the shaming of the person in active addiction. I had to ask myself, *How is this serving anyone?* and came to the conclusion that it is not. Maybe I simply have not found the perfect fit when it comes to meetings, and for that reason, I am still open to learn more.

Again, if you have found a meeting with a great leader who can support getting your addict clean, that is great news. I encourage you to stick with it. There are many paths to recovery, and for some, meetings are an effective one.

Now would be a good time to reflect on your own journey with meetings. List what you felt worked, what you feel fell short, and what you believe would be beneficial moving forward in your area.

Remember, you are still building upon your own story as an outside observer, and this is where clarity can be gained.

MEMOIR OF THE DIARIST

Journal your thoughts in the space below.

WHEN DEATH COMES KNOCKING

Death and life are nothing more than a mark in time.

The transitional phase for the soul and where Death becomes the doorway for the soul to return home to Source.

This is where the soul can renew itself once more, as each human life has a beginning and an ending.

Death equals life, and where the soul continues to live on for an eternity.

Each soul who passes on will carry all lessons learned, and where the threads of existence remain with the living.

Channeled June 2, 2018

The thing we are most afraid of, when it comes to our addict, is death and how we would survive it. This is a reality that far too many families have experienced, each person processing it at their own pace.

When we lose someone to physical death, our hearts are wounded. For some, sorrow and grief become lifetime companions. Why? Because processing the death has never found its ending.

This is where people can become temporarily blinded by their loss. They will continue to dwell in that loss and begin to miss the physical contact with that person. This is where they may begin to wonder, *Did they know how much I loved them?* If you think about it, that loss happened, not when they died, but when they were alive and in active addiction. We just found a way to deal with it then, because there was always the hope of recovery. We never imagined it would become a permanent ending.

I want to share a story with you about my husband's side of the family. His younger brother was an addict, and it was his brother's drug of choice that took his life in the 1980s. You see, the Dragon has been around for quite some time now, and so many families have been affected by his influence. All of the names in this story will not be revealed out of respect for the family, but the story is very important because it covers generational addiction. Three generations, to be exact.

Shortly after we were married in 1991, my husband began reminiscing about his childhood. It was during this time that he told me he'd had a younger brother who passed away from a drug overdose. Generational addiction flooding into his awareness.

My husband looked me in the eyes and said, "My brother, Tommy, would have really liked you."

My guy was the second of three rough-and-tumble boys, always getting into adventures that would make you laugh. They were a tight-knit crew, and if one brother was in trouble, the other two wouldn't be far behind to lend a helping hand, or even a fist or two.

The boy's spent their summers waterskiing on the Chain of Lakes and boating with their father Chuck. During the summer break, he would bring them along to the auto parts store in Chicago, where he worked. He even allowed his boys to drive and deliver auto parts. The joy for a ten-year-old boy sparkled in my husband's eyes. He fondly recalled driving through the back alleys of the city, sitting on a stack of catalogs so he could see over the steering wheel. He told me that when they stayed at his dad's house, they lived on filets and lobster tails; Chuck was never shy about living life to its fullest. Indeed, it sounded like a great childhood.

There were also other stories that included Chuck's drinking. Here is one that comes to mind. When Chuck got too drunk to drive, he allowed his children to do the driving for him. One of the boys would sit on their father's lap and steer the car. I was told that Chuck would run the pedals because their legs were too short to reach the floorboard. As they went through the tollbooth, the attendants stared in disbelief as one of the boys handed them change to pay the toll. As you can see, alcohol can be just as deadly as heroin. When consumed in excess, it becomes a different way to feed the Dragon.

My husband went on to reveal that his younger brother's problem with drugs began as a pre-teen. He told me that he started finding drug paraphernalia in his twelve-year-old brother's bedroom. When he tried to tell their mother, she just blew it off. I could only imagine, that like the rest of us, she was probably in denial about her baby's drug addiction at the time.

"My brother was cool," my husband said, "but different than I was." He recalled how their choices led them down different pathways. My husband's choices led him to learn a trade by enlisting in the military; his brother stayed the course, and in active addiction.

Even after time had passed, I could still see that his love for his brother was still very much alive within his heart.

In 1982, my husband was serving in Germany when he got the call. His younger brother had died from a drug overdose. Like my husband, Tommy was married and the father of a brand-new baby girl.

My husband flew home to say goodbye and to be with the family. They gathered together on their dad's boat, spreading his ashes over the water on the Chain of Lakes. The place that held such precious memories of three young boys and their father.

From what I was told, it was a devastating loss for the family, with each parent handling it in their own way. Chuck, who continued living in the house where his son had died, sunk even deeper into the pit, with alcohol fueling his descent. His mother carried the guilt about her son's death until she passed away. Both continued to blame the other for their son's death, which consumed the remainder of their own lives.

Years later, I sat down with Gram, my husband's grandmother, and we talked about death, loss, and moving forward.

Chuck had just passed away, his years of alcohol abuse certainly a contributing factor. We were all trying to move through that painful time together as a family.

Gram and I had spent many nights chatting at her kitchen table. On this particular evening, I asked her, "How do you do it? How have you moved through life after so much loss and with such grace?"

She looked me straight in the eye and said, *You have to stay strong for the living. What good will it do to dwell in the things we cannot change?* She smiled softly, wiped a tear from her eye, and sipped her coffee. We never spoke of this again.

You see, Gram had endured more loss than anyone I have ever known. Some of it was connected to addiction. Not only had she outlived all of her siblings; she had outlived both of her children and four of her grandchildren. It was during this conversation that I came to see that her experience with death was filled with the knowledge of living.

This is a story of generational addiction; Both of Gram's children had each lost a child of their own, then used alcohol to numb their pain. That alcohol abuse eventually led to their deaths.

Gram's wisdom is an important part of this story. She was a woman weathered by loss, grief, and the ability to persevere through it all. As an outside observer, she watched the people closest to her pass away. The connection to each passing was, at times, a connection to addiction. Her strength and resolve carried her forward in life. Her love for these same family members never wavered, even despite what some would call their shortcomings. We can all learn so much from Grams' story.

Every person living has a battle they are fighting or have fought. It is what we all have in common. The only difference is in the way we handle those battles. Take a moment to see where your own mind dwells. Write those thoughts down. This will shine a light on how you have handled those storms in life.

If you have lost someone to addiction, you might take some comfort in the fact that the addict is no longer fighting. This is where you are given an opportunity to make peace with their death and heal yourself from your loss. I have been guided to understand that when a person sheds their physical body, it is just as beautiful as when they were born into this world. This is where they are encompassed in the light of love, free from the addiction that had consumed them. Free from the pain they were trying to numb. Free from the burdens in a world filled with possibilities and the unknown.

You must remember that the journey of the soul is eternal, and this was just one stop along the way. To us, death may feel so final, but to the souls who have passed on, it is like a breath of fresh air as they are welcomed home once again.

The lessons on both sides of addiction are those we were meant to go through and learn from. There is always another person just around the corner in active addiction. This is where you can utilize your knowledge and be in service to others.

If you were to meet an outside observer or even an addict right now, what could you teach them, from your experience, to help them see a future beyond the Dragon's influence?

This is where you become empowered to recognize that your own addict's life was not in vain. It's an opportunity to learn about unconditional love, free will, and healing through loss. This is where you realize that you must stay strong for the living, as they need you more than you could ever realize.

Now is a great opportunity to write down your thoughts while they are fresh in your memory. The healing process takes time, and the effort put in by you now will pay off in dividends if applied.

MEMOIR OF THE DIARIST

Journal your thoughts in the space below.

THE CHILDREN OF ADDICTS

Thinking about Gram reminded me about the unique and strong bond between grandparents and grandchildren, and how addiction impacts this bond. I am aware that I am not the only parent or grandparent to raise the children of an addict. As I sat with this knowledge, I felt it was important to shed some light on these little ones, who are feeling the loss of love from that maternal or paternal guidepost.

As I share a bit of wisdom, encouragement, and light, my hope is that it will allow you to see the importance of giving these children a stable environment to grow within. As you each navigate the pathway as an outside observer, and now raising your grandchildren, do it from a place of love, peace, and experience. Remain mindful of this: the kids are the ones left without a parent. It is also where we become separated from our own child due to their addiction.

Either through active addiction or actual death, everyone has experienced a loss in this instance.

This is where you must dig deep and find courage in the face of adversity. Even when it feels impossible, stand firm in the strength of your convictions while utilizing your own wisdom to back it up. Yes, this is easier said than done, but I promise you it can be achieved.

I am also aware that some may not be up to the task of raising their kids' children. It is, after all, not a requirement of the outside observer. However, many are faced with the same decision about what will happen to those children if we don't step in.

This is an individual decision that each of us must navigate from our own vantage point. There is no right or wrong here, as the stage has been set by the addict. It is, after all, the decisions that have been made by them, that have put everyone involved in a very tough situation. In the end, you also must be true to yourselves in the process. If you are not, no one benefits, and the cycle of addiction can prevail as these little ones emulate the addict that they love.

This is a great opportunity to look a bit deeper at the cycle of addiction in the family unit. Take a moment and reflect on whether it is generational or not. This way, you will have a firm understanding of what needs to change for the sake of the children moving forward. Don't forget to write down your reflections as they become a guidepost in your own healing.

Now, some may be wondering, how can we save the kids when we are struggling ourselves? The answer is simple: be the light upon the pathway for your children to follow. This simply means: become the leader of your pack. It is not fair to the kids to sit idle and watch them wither away. If you choose this path, it will become a labor of love, and one that will give you the strength to persevere.

It is when we step into the impossible, where we can then toss a lifeline to those who are unable to care for themselves just yet.

As an outside observer, we have crossed many bridges to save our addicts from drowning. It is when they don't care to be saved that we step in for the sake of the kids.

Moving forward, we must try to teach these kids from a place of experience. This is where we can validate them, and allow them to know that they are still loved through it all. You must also find a way to answer those hard questions when they get old enough to ask. This is not about bashing the addict, but rather about seizing the opportunity to teach the children about acceptance, to show them compassion, and to guide them through a very difficult situation.

Your words will become like a trail of breadcrumbs home, where they can feel safe even though they may be scared. They may be hard to reach at times, as they are navigating a world without Mom or Dad in it. When they drop their shields and open their tiny hearts to you, it becomes a new beginning for you both.

Being a parent is hard; however, being a parent to your grandchildren can be a blessing. It is where you can take what may not have worked with your own kids in the past and make the changes that will allow your family to flourish. This is where you can reflect on what you have learned along the way and adjust accordingly moving forward.

Allow me to close with some wisdom.

The River of Tears

As the tears of their sorrows feed the river before them, you must continue to nurture them from the waters of your infinite knowledge and wisdom.

For when you feed them from your soul's light, they
shall never go hungry. But starve them from your ego
and they will seek outside of your home for shelter.

Love can, and will, break any barrier before it, for
love is the healer of all souls.

Channeled January 23, 2014

In the end, remember this: the keys to raising a family come from the experiences that you have already lived, and it is from this place of wisdom that you become the teacher for those tiny ears to hear.

MEMOIR OF THE DIARIST

Journal your thoughts in the space below.

ENLIGHTENMENT FROM
THE OTHER SIDE OF LIFE

I thought this would be a good time to share with you a story from my time as a working medium. It is about the impact of sudden death. Many families of addicts have experienced this, and I thought this message would bring some comfort.

It was June 3, 2018, one of those evenings when, after a mediumship demonstration, I always came home a bit more enlightened.

On this night, a spirit husband and father came forward to speak to his family, while also addressing the whole group about death. He shared what happens when the human body experiences a life-ending impact. He told us that the soul immediately leaves the body and experiences no pain.

He went on to say that the silver cord is immediately cut, and the only pain experienced is by the living. He said, that the people left behind experience a pain that can become all-consuming.

He then asked his wife to let go of her grief. He imparted that she needed to move forward because she needed to be strong for their children.

He told her that by letting go of her grief, she could enjoy the life she had left.

What a beautiful message this was. I am sure it is so very hard for a grieving widow to just let go; however, as he spoke these words of wisdom to her, I watched her energy shift. This is where I could see some of her pain melting away.

In my opinion, this is what mediumship is all about: helping to heal the hearts of the sorrowful, so that they can find peace in the passing of a loved one.

Please know that the evidence given during a mediumship reading does validate a life once lived. This becomes the proof that there is life after death, and that death is only the birth of the soul back to Source.

So for you, the outside observer, spend some time with these words. Focus on the message given so that you can heal those broken pieces within you. This is when one simple message for one family can become universal in nature. It is where the wisdom becomes the salve upon the hearts of the grieving and gives hope in the land of the living.

This is where you can honor your addict's life and reminisce in the memories that can make you smile. It is where you can let go of the sadness and realize that some people are in our lives for a season, a reason, or a lifetime. This includes our family members as well.

MEMOIR OF THE DIARIST

Journal your thoughts in the space below.

CUTTING THE CORD OF ENABLING

When our children suffer, so do we. When they are facing difficult moments in life, we do too.

When our children travel down a road that leads to a dead end, we stand beside them, hoping that they will see the wall that is right before them. We try to lead them back to the crossroads of choice, only to find ourselves back at the dead end of active addiction. We hope and pray that they see the error of their ways as we gently take their hand and lead them home. We have not realized, just yet, that this is causing more harm than good during those painful moments.

I have heard people say that this is enabling a child. I was told to let them fall until they learn. I say, until you walk a mile in my shoes, you have no idea what it is like to be a witness to active addiction. I had to learn that the fall is important for the addict, yet through enabling, the outside observer continues to be the break in that fall.

The enabler in you may think, "It's my baby, how could I not want to save them?" As a parent myself, I do understand. In most cases, it's just too painful to watch from the sidelines. Yet, what is a parent to do?

How do they shut off a heart filled with love for a child that they have known since birth? This is where the work done by you now is important moving forward. Not only for yourself, but for your addict as well. So, let's begin.

What do you consider "enabling" to be?

Is giving your child a second, third, or even fourth chance a bad thing to do?

Do you leave the porch light on, and the door unlocked so they can return to the safe haven of your home?

Answering these questions will give you some clarity about your addict, along with your part in things. What you are honest about here today, will be helpful for the outside observer moving forward.

From a spiritual standpoint, you will benefit as you engage your own intuition, while opening up a new doorway on perspective. This is where you can begin to shed some light on those dark moments. This is where you can become the beacon, a lighthouse, a source of wisdom. This is how you can help to heal a family while making yourselves whole once again.

Spirituality comes in many forms, and this my friend, is where you become the student. It prepares you to become the teacher of the wisdom gathered through your own personal experience.

When you have learned, conquered, and overcome, a torch is ignited. This torch is kindled by the lessons learned along the way. It stays lit through the work done by you now. It prepares you to pass the torch onto others. It becomes a source of hope for those who are now standing where you once stood.

First and foremost, the gift of awakening is for yourself. What is born from that gift becomes an eternal flame of knowledge.

MEMOIR OF THE DIARIST

Journal your thoughts in the space below.

I OFFER YOU A HELPING HAND

Each person is on a solo ride in the evolution of their own soul.

Each person walks an independent pathway toward enlightenment.

Each person has the power to choose and the free will to accept what each choice will bring to them.

Each person is, after all, an independent thinker with the power to manifest the life that they desire.

The experiences, the trials, the successes are all created by each person's need, and through the choices that they have made.

Each person deserves love, acceptance, and even a second chance.

We may never know what each person has gone through, the mountains that they may have climbed, the bridges that they may have crossed.

We may never know what has been stamped upon their own heart center.

But looking beyond the surface layer of each person's present moment becomes the gift.

It is from this place of understanding that the strong become the example for the weak, and where a hand is extended to each person in need.

It is from this perspective of what doesn't break you only makes you stronger.

This is for the misunderstood, the person in need of that hand-up, and where the best part of each person involved rises to the surface.

It is from this place of understanding where all people are supported, nurtured and loved. It is within this energy that evolution and enlightenment become the beacon of hope for all.

Channeled and Inspired Writing,
November 24, 2018

Author's Reflections

This beautiful passage encompasses space for the addict and the outside observer.

Each one reaching in their time of need.

Each one looking for that light in a darkened room.

Each one still holding onto hope that tomorrow will be a better day.

If you could take a moment and look at yourself first, where do you find yourself in this wisdom?

Next, where does your addict hold space?

Finally, where do the roads intersect for you both?

MEMOIR OF THE DIARIST

Journal your thoughts in the space below.

ADOPTING SPIRITUAL PRACTICES

There is more to your spiritual journey than meets the eye. In order to grow spiritually, you must invoke daily spiritual practices.

Some practices can be finding time for prayer, daily gratitude, journaling, or even meditation. These simple practices can change how you move through life. If you can begin with one, you will grow into others. The first step is always important. It is simply up to you to follow what you are drawn to do.

Whether you are a beginner or an advanced student, we all need a reminder that being centered is what creates balance.

I would suggest that you begin with the practice of journaling. The cool thing is, that you are actually learning how as you navigate this book. By putting your feelings onto paper, you are releasing them so that they no longer consume you daily. It is like giving it to God, and allowing yourself an opportunity to be heard.

I found that journaling your "gratitudes" for example, is a great way to honor yourself. If you do this for 30 days straight, it will shift your own energy. I have done this for myself and experienced the benefits of gratitude's gift. I know that we can all find something to be grateful for, even when we are in the midst of surviving our loved one's addiction.

Each day, begin by writing, "I Am grateful for..." followed by the good in your life. It can be something as simple as, "I Am grateful for this beautiful day." Begin with three things a day, and by the end of the 30 days you'll find yourself listing more.

Journaling will become a staple in your life, and much like breathwork, it can be cathartic. This is where you create space for the spiritual heart to grow. The heart needs a loving environment, and this is how you provide yourself one.

I also suggest learning how to meditate. You don't have to spend an hour a day on meditation. Even closing your eyes for five minutes daily will benefit you on a soul level. Just quiet the mind and allow that peaceful, easy feeling to move in.

Prayer is another way to move into a state of meditation or grace, if you will. By focusing on the prayers said, you give yourself time to quiet the outside world during that time.

Creating a daily discipline for yourself has many benefits. For the outside observer, quieting the mind's chatter is critical. It gives you an opportunity to gain a sense of control in the chaos of dealing with active addiction.

SELF-WORK EQUALS SELF-WORTH

When we strive to be anything, we must first do the work internally so that we can be of service externally. This is called mindful action.

Spiritual development is only a piece of the puzzle. To truly encompass your spiritual nature, work is required on your part. This is where the Self-Work Equals Self-Worth comes into play.

This simply means that if we do not work on the full development of self first, then anything we do external of ourselves will only fall flat. It's like baking a cake; if you rush the process, the cake will fall and never rise to perfection. This is when you can create an empty feeling inside of yourself and just give up.

Recognizing the importance of developing a relationship with yourself is only a piece of the pie. After all, there are two aspects to this development. One is physical (self-work), the other spiritual (self-worth).

The rest becomes a labor of love as you navigate your way toward inner peace.

Self-development is where the building blocks are put into place. This requires you to become disciplined in your daily practices. This is where you replace the old way of thinking and living, as you step into your truth. When you do this, you build a rapport with your own intuitive nudges. This is when you become mindful of your place within the work and allow the spiritual development of self to be front and center in your daily lives.

It is a balancing act, after all, and where you will begin to recognize the difference within your own life. This is where you will learn to place one foot on your physical life path and the other on the spiritual path that encompasses the Divine within you. This is how you create a space where your own internal light will have a place to shine fully within your daily life.

Being an outside observer, and living within the energy of active addiction, has created stagnation on all fronts. The only way to get the water moving again is to begin moving yourself. When you begin to understand that the addict will have to do their own work, you give yourself the opportunity to fix you.

Let me be frank here.

If you are developing for reasons other than for the development of self, you might as well continue to throw your hands in the air in frustration. You cannot be doing it for the addict or anyone else for that matter. The only way to move forward is to recognize that you are in charge of you!

It is time we stop sugarcoating this truth!

Development only happens when a person is truly ready. When you are being nudged, are you listening? Where is the nudge coming from? Who is the nudge for? The answers are simple, yet when the outside observer is not truly aligned with their own inner knowing, all is for naught. Journal the answers to these simple questions and move on.

This is the time to reinforce the foundation beneath your own two feet. It is key to the building blocks of inner peace. If you aren't prepared to fight back, then your house will never truly be built.

This is how you stop the Dragon and remove yourself from this war. To **achieve** inner peace, you must **desire** inner peace.

MEMOIR OF THE DIARIST

Journal your thoughts in the space below.

TEMPER THE EGO

Temper the ego and you temper the tongue.

For an ego that is out of balance will become like an out-of-control child with no boundaries or discipline, as the balance within has not yet been achieved.

You see dear ones, everything in life has its place, even the ego.

When the adjustments are made, you soften the abrasive side of the human condition.

For the ego must recede, so that balance can be achieved, to allow the softness of your spirit to be seen.

Channeled March 5, 2015

Author's Reflections

This is a message that speaks to the hearts of those who cannot see beyond their own noses (i.e., the addict). As the errors of their ways are given free rein, they become the dominant force around them.

The outside observer can also fall into this category and must be mindful of the ego's influence.

When the ego is out of balance, this is when we become our own worst enemy. It is where we can begin to repel people and experiences from us, instead of drawing them in.

Sound familiar? This is exactly what the addict has created and what the family as a whole experiences through them.

The pitfalls are very clear. Yet, when we can only see red, we tend to fall right in.

When we find ourselves in this situation, it is best to stop, even for a moment, and correct our course of action. This tiny little step can be so powerful if utilized in those red moments. This is how balance can be restored and maintained.

The daily practice of mindfulness is where the balance in life is achieved. The passage below will give you a peek into this wisdom.

The Importance of Mindfulness

Life will deliver you to many doorways.

Some will feel like home, yet others are not so welcoming.

It is by choice which doorways to walk through and which ones you respectfully walk away from. Yet each threshold holds a lesson for your souls' growth.

Get trapped not by the human condition as it can become a maze of twists and turns, spinning you one way only to lead you backward in time.

The harder the lesson, the longer you will be lost until you surrender and allow. It is only through choice that you will close the door behind you.

Please know that each doorway you stand before is a part of your inherited destiny.

Feel the texture of each door presented to you before you enter it, as the key to the experience is revealed through your touch.

Channeled October 30, 2014

BLISS IS A STATE OF MIND

In this lifetime we are given the opportunity to live within the parameters of peace while floating in the sea of harmony. When accomplished, I can only explain the feeling as bliss. How we get there is through disciplined action. How we achieve the state of bliss is through balance.

This is not always easy when we are exposed to active addiction. Yet I cannot stress enough about the importance of self-care. Remember, it is okay to feel joy for yourself, even when you see others suffering. The key is mindfulness and recognizing the triggers that pull you away from your joy.

Two choices, one outcome.

1. Being blessed with free will allows us to immerse ourselves in the drama of this lifetime.
2. Become a good steward of our own peace and float in the practice of mindfulness.

As you can see, these two are the opposite sides of the same energy, and that true balance is found in the middle.

1. Free Will over Mindfulness.
2. Chaos versus Peace.

These are two great examples of choices that can be made. The key is being mindful when choosing.

If you find yourself easily nudged toward the drama, pay attention to "Who" has been allowed to disrupt your peace. There are two choices to be made, and they are always made by you.

1. You can participate.
2. You can walk away.

As you have come to see, living with an addict is full of twists and turns, peace and drama, ups and downs. It is finding the balance between the positive and the negative, so that the light of peace can shine upon you.

We are each given ample opportunities to make the appropriate decisions. It is always about who we let in and who we let pass us by. This is achieved through trial and error. There may come a time in your life when solitude is necessary to make the appropriate choices. This is why you must learn to go internal and seek for those answers. Remain mindful that nothing external of yourself can validate who you are as a person, unless you allow it to be.

When dealing with a person in active addiction, ask yourself this question: are they contributing to your bliss, or are they stealing your joy?

This is a great time to make a journal entry and continue building upon your story.

MEMOIR OF THE DIARIST

Journal your thoughts in the space below.

EMBRACE LIFE TO THE FULLEST

Even in your darkest moments, each opportunity has been given its own light.

This light becomes a guidepost, an awakening for you to fulfill that portion of your destiny.

Yet, it is up to the seeker of this light, to experience the wisdom of what God's light has to offer.

Channeled on December 17, 2014

Author's Reflections

This passage speaks to our personal choices when dealing with an addict. As you may have noticed, your own light can become dimmed when intertwined with theirs.

It is our worry, our fear, our own anger at times, that dims our pathway toward our destined moments in life.

Yet the light within this darkness is where wisdom is gained.

When active addiction is present within our lives, we tend to put our dreams and desires on hold. This is where the Wisdom of God's voice is silenced for a time.

Navigating this journey can make you feel isolated. The only way out is to step away from that which has consumed you.

Free will has its place in all things, even the steps that will take you toward the light.

THE IMPORTANCE OF
JOURNALING

There are two important tools to be used as you travel down this spiritual path of healing.

The first is you; yes, you. This is where you show up and commit to the process of reconnecting to your own Divine spark. You see those that journal daily open themselves up to a deeper form of communication with self. This is truly where the healing can begin for the outside observer and even the addict.

Second is your journal. It is important to journal about your life, along with your spiritual experiences. It is through your own hand that the record is created.

It doesn't have to be anything special with any type of ritual involved. It just becomes a space that you make time to participate in.

The more you make time, the deeper you dive in. As mentioned earlier, a great way to begin is by writing down what you are grateful for today. It can be as simple as I Am grateful for the morning sunlight, too, I Am grateful for my many blessings including my addict.

If you can find the time daily to sit in silence and learn to receive, your daily practice will become a desire. This even opens the pathway to sitting in meditation much easier, especially for the novice.

For today, be still for five minutes and just listen.

What is it that you hear, see, or even feel? Write it down in your journal. This is your soul's voice, calling to be heard as the wisdom of this internal part of yourself is revealed.

Don't discount your thoughts as crazy. Validate them, and the internal beauty of self will also be validated, recorded, and heard like never before.

MEMOIR OF THE DIARIST

Journal your thoughts in the space below.

LEARN TO MEDITATE

There is a great benefit for us when we learn the art of meditation, as it rejuvenates the body, mind, and spirit.

Through the practice of meditation, we learn to release control of all things outside of ourselves as we shift our focus and go internal. It is in these moments that we allow ourselves to be fully immersed in the experience, and through this practice we can learn to apply the same principles to our everyday lives.

The benefits of meditation are many. It can teach us how to find balance, especially when we are in the midst of the Dragon's den.

During meditation, you will bring forth a sense of balance to the body, mind, spirit. This is where peace and harmony begin to become more fully present and woven into the fabric of your everyday experience.

It is through the art of meditation that you will learn to tune into that higher guidance as you begin the practice of quieting the thinking mind. When you achieve that state of quiet, you allow your spirit to soar as you go direct and connect with Source.

For those new to meditation, there are many methods you can utilize to bring yourself into that state of being. From music and guided meditations, to walking in nature or sitting in silence, the roads inward are plentiful.

This is only the beginning of things to come. When you become well-versed and disciplined in your practice of meditation, you will have a stronger connection to your own intuition. This is when you can begin to build a bond with your own internal wisdom.

Give meditation a try by quieting the mind, relaxing the body, and allowing your spirit a place to grow. Focus on your breath; it becomes a pathway inward. This is where you can connect to the wisdom of your soul's voice through the art of meditation.

When you can quiet the chatter of the everyday world around you, it is then that you can hear clearly the sound of wisdom as it is whispered on the wind."

Channeled January 30, 2016

I am going to include the links to a couple of guided meditations that I have for sale online. They are a great resource and can help you learn to meditate through channeled words of wisdom.

All are available on Amazon Digital Music

1. *Awaken to the Beauty of Your Own Inner Light Guided Meditation* by Patricia Horton
2. *Reflections of Body Mind Spirit Guided Meditation* by Patricia Horton

3. *Journey into the Magic Mirror Guided* Meditation by Patricia Horton

Let's close this section out with a bit of wisdom on meditation.

The Seekers of Wisdom

For the seekers of your world, know this: when you are ready, we are waiting.

For as you desire to work with us, we too desire to work with you.

All that is asked of you is to sit in the seat of meditation.

When you do, please do it with an open mind and a loving heart. This is where we are given the opportunity to whisper in your ear, while you grow your spirit.

Doubt not what is given, yet be open to receive it and apply this wisdom to your everyday life.

For you are an infinite vessel of knowledge yourself.

We are just the guardians of your innate wisdom and assist in amplifying the sound of your own soul's voice.

Know that your Soul is Eternal.

As you draw from the depths of your own wellspring of knowledge, apply that which is needed and will benefit you most in this lifetime.

Beautiful souls of light are you. Please know that it is our privilege to be your guide.

Meditation, Meditation, Meditation.

Channeled on December 5, 2014

Author's Reflections

The benefits of meditation are many, including connecting with God's Divine Wisdom.

Your soul's voice is also the place where God's voice is whispered from within you.

The gifts of the spirit await you!!! All you have to do is commit and allow.

The more you sit in the seat of meditation, the stronger your connection will be. This is when the information will just flow.

You may see visions, hear a voice, or even experience a feeling. All of those things are normal as you tap into this experience.

Meditation is, after all, a discipline. And, like anything else in life, the more that you apply yourselves to the practice, the easier it will become.

Meditation should never create fear within you, and it is not a requirement, just a suggestion.

If your desire is to discover your own innate wisdom, this is just one of the many benefits.

Please know this: that when you make time for meditation, you are making time for your soul's voice to be heard.

CENTER YOURSELF

Centering yourself and learning to be in your own power is important.

For when harnessed, you open yourself up to your own potential.

The power source that lies deep within your center is accessed through the journey of silence.

For you must quiet the thinking mind in order to hear its voice.

To feel its power re-enforces the importance of the journey.

Your power center is the home of your unspoken truth, and when accessed it speaks volumes.

Take this journey daily to the center of your soul's light.

As you do, you will see, feel, and hear the voice of the power that resides within you.

Channeled November 11, 2014

Author's Reflections

This message is twofold, and it speaks to the practice of meditation. This is the space where you can access the voice of your own soul's wisdom.

This is where you can detach from the hold the addict has over your life. It is a way to create a new avenue through one of the many spiritual practices.

Silence over Chaos equals Peace for you.

To hear this voice, you need to journey inward. The key is letting go of all outside distractions and learning to just be. This is what I would call letting go and allowing God.

When you can truly let go, you will see how your center becomes one of many pathways that can lead you to those destined moments in life.

The soul holds the answers to the mysteries of your life. Yet the only true way to get to the answers is to travel inward.

The pathway inward is to quiet the thinking mind and journey. When your center is accessed, you step into your own power.

Jesus taught His own disciples the importance of the journey, so they could hear and communicate with the Father. He also used prayer as a pathway toward enlightenment.

Finally, it is through practice and dedication that a deeper spiritual experience awaits you.

Getting up close and intimate with your own soul is a blessing. It will connect you with God's Divine Wisdom and what will serve you best. This is, after all, the most beautiful place to be.

EVOLUTION OF THE ADDICT

We each have something of value to share with others, and as one person seeks, another person gives.

This is where humanity grows as a collective whole and where souls unite to awaken the masses.

There are no mistakes, no chance meetings as Divine intervention lends a hand to each soul who is seeking.

Our course in life is predetermined before we incarnate. Each person we encounter becomes a point of light in time, and within our own journey of learning.

The beauty of a lifetime lived is that we are fully supported in our own endeavors. This is where we move about, opening doors to a multitude of experiences.

Each person alive is surrounded by what is called our soul group, and each person has the task of assisting in the evolution of another soul's journey.

Be joyful weary traveler, as the beauty of a lifetime lived unfolds before you.

*Let not the physical form become the deterrent to
realize the gift of this incarnation.*

Allow the body to lead you to what you have need of.

*Your individuality becomes a gift to the experiences
chosen in the course of what you call evolution.*

Channeled and Inspired Writing April 21, 2018

Author's Reflections

This in my opinion is what meetings can offer the addict. A pathway forward to understanding and recognizing their own Divine purpose.

When the leaders have healed themselves from the same sickness, they then become the example of its experience through wisdom.

As I see it, we are all the same. Seeking answers from those who have once stood where we stand now.

It is through the answers given, where the Divine spark of light is born of the same source.

SCARS OF DELIVERANCE

For the Addict and the Outside Observer

It is through your scars that you have been delivered, to where you find yourself at today.

Old wounds have healed over, holding memories of your yesterday.

Becoming the reminder of how you have lived, learned, and grown, we pray.

Your scars are elevating your light, illumination is the way.

This battlefield defines your strength, you have never surrendered, not one precious day.

When you are faced with a reminder and the past haunts your day.

Place your hand over the scars and ask, please show me the way.

When you feel the scar's presence beating just beneath the surface.

Thank them for allowing you to evolve and for God's Grace I pray.

Inspired Writing February 28, 2016

MOVING FORWARD

I have given you much to think about, and a pathway forward if you choose to follow it.

This book was never about curing your addict. It was about helping you to understand where you both stand in the Dragon's game. By understanding the mind of the addict, and your reaction to them, you now hold the power to change the game.

The Dragon has such a hold over the addict that it can feel like the game will never end. In some cases, it doesn't; in others, a winner emerges from the ashes.

Like all outside observers, you have run the gamut of emotions: sadness, denial, anger, acceptance. Recognizing that you cannot change the addict, and finding a way to assimilate to that reality, is the ultimate prize for the outside observer.

Some of you will apply the tools shared. There are also some who may not be ready just yet. You can always revisit the guidance given when you are ready to take control of your own lives.

Those who see the value of working on yourselves will gain a sense of balance. Now, it doesn't mean that you won't fall backward, but it does give you an opportunity to find clarity in the midst of chaos.

The spiritual pathway shared will give you a place to return to when things feel out of control. And, with any addict, out of control has become the norm for far too long.

It is ultimately up to you to establish a life of your own. It is not that your addict won't be a part of your life moving forward. It is just how you allow or not allow them to disrupt your own pathway towards peace, and healing for self.

THE SIMPLE PATH

For the Addict and The Outside Observer

It is through the simplicity of life that you learn and grow the most. As you raise the white flag and lay down your sword of resistance, you can then surrender and allow.

You see, it is in the surrendering that you give way to the resistance and control regained.

As you open this doorway, you then allow your own true divinity to shine through.

There are far too many who have not understood this simple rule of thumb.

Simplicity is the only true path to enlightenment, guided through your own inner knowing.

This is how you peacefully awaken to your own soul's truth.

The simple path teaches that you do not have to do, to be. Understanding this truth is where the seeker will gain much ground.

For it is the simple path that will always guide you home, returning you to center once more.

Know that when you hold the sword of resistance within your own hands, you have then veered away from the path of simplicity, and all that it has to offer to thee.

Channeled on April 24, 2016

Author's Reflections

This passage is all about the fight and who will be the last man or woman standing.

It also teaches you about the importance of surrendering.

In the fight between addiction and sobriety, the addict versus the outside observer, someone will have to concede.

This someone will be you, until the addict is willing to surrender to their own vices.

For your own sanity, wave the white flag and walk away from the battle. This is when true change can occur for all parties involved.

How do you feel about this course of action? Write your thoughts down as it becomes a part of your story, and a lesson for you to learn from.

MEMOIR OF THE DIARIST

Journal your thoughts in the space below.

LOVE LETTERS

A Letter from my Addict

Dear Grandma,

Thank you so much for everything you do for me. Thank you for raising me and teaching me right from wrong. I want you to know that you did everything right raising me. I chose to do wrong on my own.

I want to make you proud and be everything you know I can be. You are the most important person in my life. You are my heart and my soul. You are the light that shines in my darkness.

You are the coolest grandma on this earth. You can talk to dead people, you have a huge sense of humor, and your amazingly smart. You have all the experience there is, and therefore I can come to you for advice about anything. Even though half the time I don't want to hear the truth, but I know it's the truth.

Thank you for always putting me first and thank you for just being you. I love you so much grandma, never forget that. If I ever die, just know that I will be around you always. Following you, moving things, haunting you.

You will always be a part of me, and I will always be a part of you.

XOXO
April 22, 2019

Author's Reflection

This was secretly written in my journal by a grandchild who today is still in active addiction. These are her words, unaltered, and shared by me.

It touched my heart and showed me they can, and do, hear us. It just may not be their time to let go of the Dragon just yet.

It showed me that I am important even when I feel as if my words are falling on deaf ears.

Never give up, as the threads of your love for your own addict have been felt, received, and even processed. They just may not be able to say them just yet.

A Letter to my Addict

Princess,

You are the light of my life, the wind in my sail, the sun on my cheeks on a warm summer day.

I have loved you for an eternity and my love for you will never die.

I can see your spirit, your strength, and your strong will. These things can serve you well if only you allow them to.

All things in their own perfect timing and through the perfection of your own life.

No judgments, just love.

No hate, just peace.

No limits, no boundaries.

Live your life and be true to who you are. This is when you will know that you have given all of us the best pieces of you.

Love always, Grandma
April 24, 2019

Author's Reflections

Looking back at this letter written in response to my addict, I can still feel the purity of my own words. The power of my love, written by an unbiased scribe.

Writing this entry in this book today helps me realize the importance of the written word. The importance of allowing myself the opportunity to capture my heart's love for a person I have known since birth.

I encourage you to write a love letter to your own addict. Capture the purity of your love and allow that love to heal what addiction has wounded.

MEMOIR OF THE DIARIST

Journal your thoughts in the space below.

WITH THE SOUL'S PERMISSION

The Soul must always give permission before outside influences can heal it from its Karma.

The lesson of Karma equals growth, and growth occurs when the lesson is ready to be rectified.

For not even those who call themselves healers can change nor influence the souls' path.

Be ever so mindful that it takes two to tango.

The dance with flesh and blood is a dance the soul will choose as its path towards enlightenment.

Channeled November 9, 2019

Author's Reflections

The journey of the addict and the outside observer are based on love, intertwined with karma. Karma becomes the sword that wounds, because to heal the karma, the war must be fought.

We were each born into this lifetime and this physical existence by choice. From your physical bodies to your current circumstances, they were all pre-planned by your soul for lessons and growth. Even addiction and the pathway toward recovery.

Nothing is by accident or chance; everything good, bad or indifferent is for your greatest good and highest joy. Even when you have to battle the Dragon.

Now, this may not sound so good if you are struggling today, but you just need to see the flip side of the coin in all of this.

Struggles can be overcome; you have the strength to do that. You may just have to dig a little bit deeper, for your soul was prepared for this exact moment in time.

This is where you can apply the tools given, the understanding gained, and where you honor your own self in the process.

There is no magic wand that can be waved. But there is magic in the shared wisdom that can transform any set of circumstances, if only you allow.

As you fight, know that we all fight this Dragon together. It is when we defeat the Dragon that we can become a teacher of the knowledge gained.

Never give up hope, keep the faith, and know that God is always within reach showing us the way.

A FINAL FAREWELL

The story of addiction seems to be a never-ending one, with different players in the Dragon's game.

No matter who they are, each addict has a story to tell, and there are people who have loved them through it all.

As I go through the final editing process of this book, I am also bidding farewell to someone special. As she moved into the final stages of her life, we did it together.

Who is she? She is a self-described alcoholic and will tell you that she has lived a fabulous life. She is a woman who is not only a hostess to all, but an example of what it means to not hide your light under a bushel.

She will tell you that between her nose and her chin is her mouth, from which her honest opinions flow freely. As I have navigated these last ten months with her, I also navigated generational addiction. This is where I understood that to not judge her had been the gift for her, and where love became the blessing for us both.

I have always believed that to be able to speak to those we love before either of us passes on is so important.

My hope is that she knew my life had been made better through her friendship. She called me a sister, and has left me knowing the value of friendship cannot be measured nor weighed.

There are so many things that I want to share with you about her. The story below is one that was experienced during the final leg of her journey, and together, it became our journey.

It sums up grace in the hour of death. This is when we were both visited by one of God's Angel's.

In the hospital together, we met a man who appeared out of nowhere. He was dressed in light blue with eyes that matched. He had wavy blond hair and a mustache that framed his mouth. He approached us both with an energy that is still to this day indescribable. It was when he spoke the full name of your sister, that his words left us stunned. He guided us to her room when nurses and hospital staff were unable to locate her. He sent us to room 222 and told us to go with an urgency. It was where Dawn was waiting for you. Her own addiction had taken its toll on her body. A final goodbye was given, a kiss on the forehead received, forgiveness and love between two sisters was witnessed by me. This gift was for both of us and one that mere words cannot describe.

A messenger angel was sent… to be a witness remarkable… as God's grace flowed freely in that short window of time. It was in those final moments that we shared something special. In that hour, we were both touched by an Angel.

Now, I had been watching the Big Dipper over your house, and I knew that soon it would scoop you up and deliver you to the heavens above. A reunion awaits you, my heart hurting as I write these words.

Time never stops moving, and your friendship is one that I will surely miss, as I continue to navigate a world without you in it.

This is my love letter to you, my dear friend, and one that fills me with many emotions, laughter, joy, and grief. You told me not to be sad, but it is impossible not to be when someone like you is lost to this world.

I will be waiting for your sign from heaven. My faith in the promise of God assures me that you are now encompassed in the light of healing, love, and grace.

Fly free, Deanne. Your friendship was a gift and one that has left me with a lifetime of memories.

R.I.P. September 19th, 2025

ABOUT THE AUTHOR

Known as the "Spirit Scribe," Patricia Horton is one of the most insightful mediums and spiritual teachers of our day. Throughout her forty-five years of doing this work, Patricia has taught, written, and channeled from a place of humility and a love of being in service to God, and all she works with.

Her philosophy is to keep it simple, and it is from this platform that those placed in her path are fed from a place of knowledge and understanding. Her intention is always to guide others toward God's Divine Light.

Patricia's passion along with a dedication to her work becomes evident to those who sit within the walls of her classroom. She is a woman of deep faith and gives all the Glory to God, for she understands it is His Divine Hand that guides her daily.

In the words channeled on November 15, 2019:

We are all Divine Pieces of God's Light, walking Individual Paths of Purpose.

Patricia invites you to explore the light within yourselves from this unique perspective.

Connect with this author on her websites:

Innereyeconnections.org or patriciahortonbooks.com